# It *Is* About You

## How American Government Works and How to Help Fix It

D1205974

## Deborah Cupples

# What You'll Get from this Book

The American government was set up to work for us, The People. Over the last few decades, it has worked less for us and more for the few who can buy influence. No doubt, parts of our system are broken.

The good news: **our government can be fixed**, and We The People can help fix it. The first step is understanding how it's supposed to work and how it's broken.

Some media and politicians try to help us understand our government. Some try to manipulate our opinions so we'll vote to protect other people's interests instead of our own.

People who know basics about our government are (1) harder to manipulate and (2) better able to help fix our system.

This plain-language, non-partisan book is in three parts:

- **Part 1:**
  – The law and your rights and duties
  – The law and our government's powers

- **Part 2:**
  – Our government's structure and limits
  – How the three branches of government operate

- **Part 3:**
  – Influences on government—some that work against us
  – Ways to help make changes

Understanding those things will help you protect your interests and influence the government to work for you. Your voice matters.

## Acknowledgements

Many thanks to the following people for helping me turn some ideas into this book (alphabetical order):

- Victorina Basauri
- Susan Carr
- Christina Coronado
- Jarid Coronado
- Cami Cupples
- Richard Goldstein
- Carol Logie
- Carl J. Olsen
- Rod Olson
- Bill Reynolds
- Melissa Rider
- Kendra Siler-Marsiglio
- Theresa Reid
- Stacey Steinberg
- Margaret Temple-Smith
- Diane Tomlinson
- Kerry Travilla-Bown

I'm also grateful to the following people for their advice, encouragement, or inspiration (alphabetical): Joel Achenbach, Gustavo Antonini, Nancy T. Baldwin, Fletcher Baldwin, Bill Cupples, Tim McShane, and Chris Morris.

# Table of Contents

| Part II | 25 |
|---|---|

**Chapter 3**    Legislative Branch: Congress
& Its Agencies .................................. 27

## Part III                                                          91

## Chapter 6     Outside Influences on Our Government
                 & Corruption of the Process.................. 93

# About the Author

Deborah Cupples is a legal-skills professor. She has taught courses involving—

- Legal document drafting

- Legislative interpretation

- Constitutional interpretation

Cupples practiced law and still does some legal consulting, including pro-bono work. She also did volunteer work for political candidates' campaigns and ran for local office.

Her formal education includes a law degree, a Master's degree in political science, and a Bachelor's degree in English. She co-authored two books relating to legal writing.

# Part I

It Starts With the Law:
Legal Basics About
You & Our Government

# Chapter 1

# Where Your Rights & Duties Come From

## The Rule of Law vs. the Rule of Men

The **Rule of Law** protects people's rights by defining government's powers through laws. The idea is to enforce the law similarly for all people—that nobody is above the law, not even presidents.

In nations under the "Rule of Men," rulers decide if the law is enforced as written. Let's say you're visiting a nation where the law says people caught texting while driving must pay a $250 fine. If that nation is under the "Rule of Men," you might be fined $250 or maybe $500. You might get a week in jail if the judge is in a bad mood or hates your haircut.

Living under the "Rule of Men" is unpredictable and unfair, like gambling in Vegas. Our Founding Fathers set up our nation under the Rule of Law because they didn't like living under a king's arbitrary and unfair use of power. They made that clear in the Declaration of Independence.

## Types of Laws: Sources of Your Rights & Duties

### Basic Overview

In the United States, our rights and duties come mostly from laws at 3 levels of government:

    (1)  The U.S. (federal) Government.

    (2)  The 50 states' governments.

    (3)  Local governments, like counties or cities, which are under each state's government.

Some Native American tribes also have some self-governance powers. So do some U.S. territories, like Puerto Rico.

Whatever level of government the laws come from, rights and duties are linked. Your right to enjoy your property is linked to other people's legal duty to not steal it.

The rest of this section covers 5 major types of laws that directly affect our rights or duties:

- Constitutions
- Statutes
- Regulations
- Local-government ordinances
- Case law

## U.S. Constitution: The Starting Point

### The Constitution's Structure

The U.S. Constitution is the starting point for your rights and freedoms. It's also the starting point for governments' powers and limits (covered in Chapter 2).

The **Framers** of the Constitution were the people who attended the Constitutional Convention in 1787 and helped write the document. For more history, check the National Archives (www.archives.gov).

The U.S. Constitution has—

- 7 major parts called "Articles"
- 27 amendments (changes)

The Constitution is in this book's Appendix, toward the end.

The U.S. Constitution is the **supreme law of the land**. Any federal, state, or local laws that violate the Constitution are unconstitutional (invalid)—after a court says so.

### The Amendments & Your Rights

The Constitution's first 10 amendments are called the **Bill of Rights**. Below is a quick list of the topics they cover:

| | |
|---|---|
| 1st: | Freedom of religion, speech, press, and assembly; right to petition government. |
| 2nd: | Right to be armed (weapons). |
| 3rd: | Right to stop soldiers from taking over people's homes in peacetime. |
| 4th: | Protection against unreasonable searches and seizures. |
| 5th: | Rights and protections regarding criminal charges and government's taking of life, liberty, and property. |
| 6th: | Rights regarding criminal trials. |
| 7th: | Rights regarding jury trials in civil cases. |
| 8th: | Protections regarding bail, fines, and cruel and unusual punishment. |
| 9th: | The People have more rights than those listed in Constitution. |
| 10th: | The states' power to pass laws. |

Only 17 other amendments were ratified (adopted) from 1795–1992. Below are the amendments after the Bill of Rights that focus on people's rights or freedoms:

| | |
|---|---|
| 13th: | No more slavery. |
| 14th: | Protection of people's Constitutional rights in the states and equal protection under the law, among other things. |
| 15th: | Right to vote regardless of person's race. |

| 18th: | Prohibition of alcohol in the U.S. |
| 19th: | Right to vote regardless of person's sex. |
| 21st: | Repeal of 18th Amendment: alcohol is legal again. |
| 24th: | Prohibition of poll taxes (charging people money to vote). |
| 26th: | Right to vote at age 18 (it was 21). |

We have more rights than are listed in the Constitution (9th Amendment). And courts' interpretations of the Constitution affect the nature of our rights.

For example, the Constitution doesn't mention the Internet, which didn't exist in the 1700s. But the U.S. Supreme Court decided that 1st Amendment free-speech and free-press rights apply to publishing things on the Internet.

The word "privacy" isn't in the Constitution, but the Supreme Court decided that certain amendments give us the right of privacy. Other rights grew out of the right of privacy, like the right to use birth control, which had been illegal in many states before the mid-1960s.

Constitutional rights are not absolute. We have free-speech rights, but governments can sometimes restrict when, where, and how we speak. For example, the police can escort someone out of a city council meeting for disrupting the event by shouting insults.

The 2nd Amendment is another example. It gives us a right to have guns, but governments can limit things like bringing guns across state lines.

Mostly, the amendments that give us rights protect us against *government* action, not private citizens' action. You would not violate the 1st Amendment by refusing to allow a drunk guest to give a speech at your birthday bash. It's your party—you can shut people up if you want to.

## Amending the Constitution Isn't Easy

Amending (changing) the Constitution is difficult, like moving the Washington Monument. That's probably a good thing because our rights and freedoms are at stake.

A *proposed* amendment can come from 2 sources:

(1) The U.S. Congress

(2) The states

Article V of the Constitution lays out details.

After an amendment is proposed, it's up to the states to ratify it or not. Ratification requires approval from 3/4 of the states' legislatures. That means thousands of people would be involved in amending the Constitution. It's not easy to get so many people to agree on every word of an amendment.

## State Constitutions

Like the U.S. Constitution, state constitutions typically address government powers and people's rights and freedoms. State constitutions can give people greater rights than the U.S. Constitution *but not lesser rights*. For example, Florida's Constitution grants people the right to use medical marijuana, but the U.S. Constitution doesn't (future legal battles could change some states' marijuana laws).

When it comes to people's rights, think of the U.S. Constitution as the floor. A state constitution can build upon the floor but can't go below it.

Different states have different processes for amending their constitution. You can find your state's constitution by searching online for "constitution" + your state.

## Statutes

### Federal Statutes

A **statute** is a law passed by a legislative (lawmaking) body. Congress is the U.S. Government's legislative body. Congress passes federal statutes, usually with the President's approval (more about Congress in Chapter 3).

The word **legislation** can refer to different things, like federal statutes, state statutes, and local government ordinances.

Statutes can give us rights or privileges. For example, statutes give authors certain rights over the books they write. Statutes entitle some people to get social security benefits.

Statutes can impose duties on people, like paying taxes. Statutes also affect the power and duties of governments (more about that in Chapter 2).

To be valid, federal statutes can't conflict with the U.S. Constitution. Federal statutes are in the **U.S. Code**, which is huge and divided into numbered **titles** that cover different topics, such as—

- **Title 2:** Congress
- **Title 18:** Crimes
- **Title 26:** Internal Revenue Code (taxes)
- **Title 52:** Voting and elections

You can find the U.S. Code online at different sites, including the U.S. House of Representatives (www.uscode.house.gov) and the Legal Information Institute (www.law.cornell.edu/uscode).

### State Statutes

A state's statutes are passed by the state's legislative body, usually with the governor's approval. Most states call their legislative body the "legislature." Some states, like Colorado and Illinois, call it "The General Assembly." New Hampshire and Massachusetts call their legislature "The General Court" (not a typo).

This book refers to any state's legislative body as a *legislature*. To find your state's legislature, search online for "legislature" + your state.

Some state statutes apply to all people in the state, even non-residents. A non-resident who commits theft while visiting Iowa could be arrested for it in that state. Some state laws apply to only residents, like laws stating how to register to vote in a state.

State statutes can't regulate things that are reserved for the federal government. For example, the U.S. Constitution gives the U.S. Government (not the states) the power to regulate patents that people get for inventions.

But states can regulate many things that aren't reserved for the federal government: the 10th Amendment says so. For example, state laws deal with drivers' licenses, marriage, and wills. States regulate many professions, like the medical and legal professions.

Different states handle issues differently through statutes. For example, California and Colorado handle divorce differently. Texas has different laws than Florida against texting while driving.

To be valid, a state statute can't violate the U.S. Constitution, U.S. statutes, or that state's constitution. States have different names for their collection of statutes, like the *Idaho Statutes*, the *California Code*, and the *General Laws of Massachusetts*. To find your state's statutes, search online for "statutes" + your state.

## Regulations

### Federal Regulations & Agencies

Federal **regulations** ("regs," for short) are rules adopted by *administrative agencies*—like the U.S. Treasury Department. Regs affect how agencies execute laws, enforce laws, and operate (more about federal agencies in Chapters 2 and 4).

For example, Congress passed statutes requiring most U.S. citizens to have passports before leaving the country. Based on statutes, the U.S. State Department set up detailed regulations for what citizens must do to get a passport.

Statutes trump regs. That makes sense because statutes give federal agencies the authority to *make* regs. Federal regs are in the Code of Federal Regulations (www.federalregister.gov).

### State Regulations

States have administrative agencies that adopt regulations. To be valid, a state's regs must not violate the U.S. Constitution, U.S. statutes, the state's constitution, or the state's statutes.

Typically, a state's collection of regs is called a **Code**, like the *Wisconsin Administrative Code* and the *Missouri Code of State Regulations*. To find your state's regs, search online for "regulations" + your state.

### Local Government Ordinances

**Ordinances** are laws passed by a local government's legislative body, like a County Commission, County Council, City Commission, City Council, etc. Two states have different names for counties: Alaska calls them "boroughs," and Louisiana calls them "parishes."

Ordinances can protect rights. For example, more than 100 cities and counties prohibit private employers from practicing employment discrimination based on gender identity.

Ordinances can also impose duties. An ordinance might limit how you can use buildings located in certain areas of a city or how late at night you can buy beer.

Local governments' powers come from state law. To be valid, local ordinances can't violate federal law or the state's law. To find your city's or county's ordinances, search online for "ordinances" + your city or county + your state.

## Case Law

Case law comes from past court cases, called **precedents**. In case law, judges write what the law requires in a certain situation. Case law exists at the federal and state levels.

Case law might involve a court's interpretation of a law. Let's say that a new state statute imposes a 5-year prison sentence on anyone who "uses a gun" while committing robbery but only 3 years if the robber doesn't use a gun.

Annie The Armed Robber had a gun in her purse while robbing Victor. She didn't threaten him with the gun. She didn't even take it out of her purse. At trial, the prosecutor argues that Annie should get 5 years because she *had* the gun and could have used it against Victor. Annie argues that she should get 3 years because she didn't actually use the gun.

In that case, the court would answer a question like this: Does the statute's 5-year sentence apply if a robber had a gun but didn't use it during the robbery? The court's answer would set a precedent for how other courts should interpret and apply that statute.

Sometimes, case law covers situations that statutes don't cover. Let's say that there's no statute about what happens if your neighbor's tree falls and crushes your car. In that case, a court might decide—based on precedents—that your neighbor owes you money to replace the car.

Precedents are crucial to the Rule of Law. Without them, judges could decide cases based on whims or absurd reasons, which would create uncertainty and unfairness (more about precedents in Chapter 5).

In many states, some areas of law are based largely on case law, like contracts and personal injury. If a legislature doesn't like the effect of certain case law, the legislature can pass statutes that override that case law.

## Exercising Your Rights

### Learning about Them

For rights to mean anything, you have to exercise them. The first step to exercising rights is *knowing* what rights you have. Let's say that you're entitled to a tax deduction for interest you paid on a loan. If you were doing your own taxes, how would you know to claim the deduction if you didn't know you were entitled to it?

The starting point for your rights is the U.S. Constitution. Whatever your political beliefs, the American Civil Liberties Union is a good source for learning about constitutional rights. Its website explains rights, like privacy, voting, immigration, and many more (www.aclu.org/know-your-rights).

Another good source is the Center for Constitutional Rights. You can browse its website (www.ccrjustice.org).

Basic online searches are another way to learn about your rights. When you have time, grab a cup of coffee and search for an issue or right + the level of government (like "U.S." or "Delaware" or "Adams County, Virginia").

Government websites tend to be reliable for government information. For example, the IRS's website has information about taxpayers' rights and duties (www.irs.gov). The Department of Veterans Affairs' website explains benefits available to veterans (www.va.gov).

Private organizations' and people's websites are a mixed bag. Some people make errors. Some people use websites to mislead visitors. Comparing multiple sources about the same right or issue can help you weed out non-credible websites.

Beefing up your knowledge of how things work doesn't guarantee that you'll always get what you want. But the more knowledge you have, the more power you'll have to exercise your rights.

## Taking Other Action

### Working out Problems

There are 2 ways to enforce your rights if a government acted against them:

(1)   Work it out with the officials involved

(2)   Work it out in court

If the Social Security Administration wrongly cut off your grandmother's benefits, she could complain to supervisors. If that fails, she could follow the agency's appeals process. At some point, she might contact a member of Congress for help (more about that in Chapter 3).

Exercising and enforcing your rights is similar at the state and local levels. If there's a problem, start with supervisors within the agency causing the problem. If that doesn't work, contact your elected representative, like a state legislator or city commissioner.

If all else fails, you could sue in court, but lawsuits usually cost money. In some cases, people whose rights are infringed might get help from legal-aid groups. You could find legal-aid groups in your area by searching online for "legal aid" + your city + your state.

### Influencing Public Policy

One way to prevent or solve problems with government agencies is to influence the public policy that guides agencies' actions. You can do that by—

• Voting for public officials who share your values

• Sharing your opinions with public officials

• Helping groups push for public policies that you like

Sometimes, influencing public policy involves short-term actions, like pressuring lawmakers to vote a certain way. Sometimes, it's a longer-term project, like helping a candidate run for office or running for office yourself. Details about your power to influence governments and help fix them are in Chapter 7.

# Chapter 2

# Sources of Federal Government Powers & Limits

**What this Chapter Covers:**

## The 3 Branches and Their Powers:

- Basic Overview
- Separation of Powers; Checks and Balances

## Laws Affecting Government Power

- U.S. Constitution
- Federal Statutes
- Federal Regulations
- Case Law

# The Three Branches & Their Powers

## Basic Overview

The federal government has 3 branches:

    (1)   Legislative Branch (Congress)

    (2)   Executive Branch (President)

    (3)   Judicial Branch (Courts)

The branches are **co-equal**, meaning no branch ranks higher than another.

The government's power is divided among the 3 branches. Congress legislates (makes laws). The Executive Branch executes and enforces laws. The Judicial Branch interprets laws. Think of it this way:

- Congress sets policies.
- The President puts the policies into effect.
- The courts play referee, deciding whether government action complies with the law.

There's more to it, which is why each branch has its own chapter in this book (Chapters 3, 4, and 5).

## Separation of Powers & Checks and Balances

**Separation of Powers** prohibits one branch of government from exercising another branch's powers. Congress doesn't enforce laws, and the President doesn't decide court cases.

The Constitution created a system of **checks and balances** partly by—

- Separating the branches' powers
- Requiring the branches to cooperate to use some shared powers

The Constitution pits the branches against each other, so each branch acts as a check on (restrains) the other branches.

Even within Congress, some power is shared. Congress is **bicameral**—divided into 2 houses, also called **chambers**:

(1)   The House of Representatives

(2)   The Senate

For Congress to pass a law, both chambers must approve.

Lawmaking is an example of checks and balances at work. Let's say that Congress passes a **bill** (a proposed law). If the President signs the bill, it becomes an actual law.

But it doesn't always work that way. The President could **veto** (reject) a bill. In that way, the President acts as a **check** against Congress's power.

But Congress could **override the veto**, and the bill would become law without the President's approval. In that way, Congress acts as a **check** against the President's power.

Even if a bill becomes law, a court could strike it down as unconstitutional. In that way, the Judicial Branch acts as a **check** against the other two branches' power.

Why such a complex system of checks and balances? Because the Framers of the Constitution wanted to protect people's freedoms, reduce the abuse of power, and promote the Rule of Law.

# Laws Affecting Government Power

## U.S. Constitution

### Basic Functions & Structure

The Constitution is a starting point for governments' powers. Basically, here's what the Constitution does regarding governments:

- Creates the federal government's 3 branches
- Assigns powers to the branches
- Addresses the relationship between the federal and state governments

Government powers and functions are covered in the Constitution's articles and some amendments. Below are topics covered by the 7 articles:

### Topics Covered by Constitution's Articles

Article I:    Legislative Branch (Congress)

Article II:    Executive Branch (President)

Article III:    Judicial Branch (Courts)

Article IV:    State-Related Issues

Article V:    How to Amend the Constitution

Article VI:    Constitution and U.S. Law are Supreme; Oaths of Office; No Religious Tests for People Qualifying for Office

Article VII:    Ratification of the Constitution

Examples of amendments that deal directly with governments' powers or functions are listed below:

- **11th:** Limits courts' jurisdiction in some lawsuits against states

- **12th:** Changes how presidents are elected

- **16th:** Gives Congress power to impose income tax

- **17th:** Allows The People (instead of the states) to elect senators

- **20th:** Sets dates when a president's and Congress's terms end; discusses presidential vacancy

- **22nd:** Sets term limits for presidents

- **23rd:** Gives Washington, D.C. electors in the Electoral College (presidential elections)

- **25th:** Creates ways to remove a president from office aside from impeachment

- **27th:** Limits pay raises for members of Congress

Chapters 3, 4, and 5 cover details about the powers and functions of the U.S. Government's branches.

### The Constitution Isn't Crystal Clear

Parts of the Constitution aren't clear. That's one reason for lawsuits about its meaning. Part of our courts' job is to interpret the Constitution (more in Chapter 5).

Parts of the Constitution lack details because it wasn't meant to micromanage everything. It contains some details, but mostly **the Constitution states broad principles** and leaves the rest for the 3 branches to hammer out.

The Constitution still applies 200+ years after it was written partly because of its broad nature. For example, airplanes didn't exist when the Constitution was written, but Congress's powers were phrased broadly enough to enable Congress to pass laws about air travel.

## Federal Statutes

Federal statutes affect governments' powers and functions. For example, the Constitution established the U.S. Supreme Court but gave Congress the power to create lower federal courts (more in Chapter 5). Congress created courts through statutes.

Congress can pass statutes about many things, as long as (1) the statute doesn't violate the Constitution and (2) Congress doesn't exceed its constitutional authority. Chapter 3 covers more about Congress's authority.

## Federal Regulations

### Types of Regulations

Administrative agencies adopt different types of regulations. Some deal with an agency's internal operations, like managing employees. Others deal with an agency's rules or procedures.

Still other regs regulate businesses' or people's conduct. For example, the Federal Trade Commission has regs that protect consumers against false advertising by businesses.

### Limits on Regulations

The Constitution trumps all other laws, including regulations. Statutes trump regs because statutes give administrative agencies the power to make regs. What Congress gives by statute, Congress can take away by statute.

The Constitution limits which tasks Congress can delegate to agencies. For example, Congress can't give agencies the power to pass statutes because the Constitution reserves that power for Congress.

Within constitutional limits, Congress can give an administrative agency broad or specific rulemaking authority. For example, Congress could direct the Department of Transportation (DOT) to set safety standards for cars and leave some details to the DOT—or Congress could be more detailed and direct the DOT to require airbags in cars.

### Rulemaking Procedures

There are formal procedures for making rules. Usually, administrative agencies publish proposed rules, so affected people know about them. Agencies often give the public a chance to comment and participate in rulemaking.

Many types of rules must be published in the Federal Register. The publication requirement promotes the Rule of Law by (1) holding agencies accountable for following proper procedures and (2) giving people notice of the regs they must follow.

As the head of the Executive Branch, the President can directly influence executive agencies' actions. Typically, presidents do that by issuing executive orders or memoranda to agency heads (more in Chapter 4).

### Case Law

Case law about the meaning of a constitutional provision, statute, or regulation can affect the government's powers and public policy. Consider Annie the Armed Robber (Chapter 1). The court's interpretation of the phrase "uses a gun" would make the difference between Annie's serving 3 years in prison or 5 years.

Case law isn't always the final word on public policy. If Congress doesn't like the outcome of a court's interpretation of a statute, Congress might change the statute to get a different outcome.

Because it's hard to change the Constitution, we tend to be stuck with a court's interpretation of it for a while. Usually, two things could change a court's interpretation of the Constitution:

    (1)  A higher court overturning a lower court's interpretation.

    (2)  A court reversing itself in later case law.

Chapter 5 covers more about courts and case law.

# Part II

## Basics about How the Government Works:

- Legislative Branch (Congress)

- Executive Branch (President)

- Judicial Branch (Courts)

# Chapter 3

# Legislative Branch:
# Congress & Its Agencies

## What this Chapter Covers:

- Members of Congress Can Help You

- Congress's Structure & Some Lingo

- House Membership, Terms, & Districts

- Senate Membership & Terms

- Congress's Powers

- Political Parties & Other Groups

- Leadership in the Chambers

- Committees

- The Legislative (Lawmaking) Process

- Legislative Branch Agencies

- Washington, D.C.—the Seat of Government

- Congress's Pay

## Members of Congress Can Help You

Members of Congress do more than make laws and raise campaign funds. Your Members represent their constituents, including you—even if you didn't vote for them.

If you live in a U.S. state, you have 3 Members of Congress: 2 senators + 1 House member. People in certain U.S. territories have one "non-voting" representative in the House.

As your representatives, your Members can do things for you. **Members *can't* help you dodge the law.** If you legally owe the IRS $500, your Members can't change that. But here are a few things they might help you with:

- Resolving issues with a federal agency (like the Social Security or Veterans Administrations).
- Resolving passport or immigration issues.
- Arranging a White House or Capitol tour.

To see what your Members can do for you, visit their official webpages through these links:

- **House:** www.house.gov
- **Senate:** www.senate.gov

On a Member's page, look for links with labels like "Assistance," "Get help," or "What Bob can do for you."

If you don't know your Members' names, search the House and Senate websites. The House search is based on your zip code, and the Senate's is based on your state.

If a Member's webpage doesn't answer your question, email or call your member's office. Here are some tips:

- Expect to deal with staff.
- Be calm and polite, whether talking or writing.
- If you need help with a problem, make contact as soon as possible so staff has time to work on it.

## Congress's Structure & Some Lingo

Congress has two chambers, also called "houses":

- The House of Representatives (lower chamber).

- The Senate (upper chamber).

"The House" is shorthand for the House of Representatives. The Senate is called "The Senate."

The House has 435 full-voting members. The bigger a state's population, the more representatives the state gets in the House. Thus, larger states have more voting power in the House.

The Senate has 100 members, and each state gets 2 of them. Thus, small states have *the same* voting power as large states in the Senate.

Typically, senators are addressed as Senator + last name (Senator Adams). For House Members, you have options:

- Representative + last name

- Congressman + last name

- Congresswoman + last name

News media often refer to Members in writing by last name + party + state:

- House Member: Rep. Adams (R-SC).

- Senator: Sen. Adams (D-NY).

For **independents**, news media use the letter "I": for example, Sen. Sanders (I-VT).

If a member of one of the other parties gets elected to Congress, a different letter would be used, like "G" for Green Party or "L" for Libertarian.

## House Membership, Terms, & Districts

House members are elected for 2-year terms, and there's no limit on how many times they can be elected. To be eligible to be a House member, a person must—

- Be at least 25 years old
- Be a U.S. citizen for at least 7 years
- Live in the state he or she represents

Those requirements are in the Constitution (Article I, Section 2).

Each state gets a share of the 435 representatives based on the state's population. In 2017, Alabama had 7 representatives in the House, and California had 53.

Most states have a big enough population to get more than one representative in the House. A **congressional district** is a geographical area in a state, as drawn by that state's government. Districts are numbered, like Iowa's 3rd District or Georgia's 4th District. Many House Members' web pages have a map of their own district.

In multi-district states, the people of each district elect one House Member. In states that have only one district, like Alaska and Vermont, the Member represents everyone in the state.

State populations can change, so the Constitution requires a population count every 10 years. It's done through the **U.S. Census**. Based on Census data, the government **reapportions** the House every 10 years—decides how many representatives each state gets based on population (Article I, Section 2).

Some states win the reapportionment game, and some lose. After the 2010 Census, Texas gained 4 House seats, and New York lost 2 seats.

Along with the 435 members from the states, the House has 6 "non-voting" members from U.S. territories:

- 5 delegates one each for American Samoa; Guam; the Northern Mariana Islands; the U.S. Virgin Islands; and Washington, D.C.

- The Resident Commissioner of Puerto Rico.

"Non-voting" members can't vote to pass a bill but can propose a bill, participate in debates, vote in committees, and represent their constituents in Washington, D.C.

## Senate Membership & Terms

Some people see the Senate as the rational adult, while the House plays the child. When the House passes ridiculous bills based on party agendas, the Senate sometimes stops the nonsense by refusing to pass them.

That doesn't mean the Senate is always like the Dalai Lama or Yoda. Some Senate leaders have acted like irrational children and dragged their party's members along.

The Senate has 100 members, 2 from each state. Both senators represent all people in their state, so there are no separate Senate districts within states. Senators are elected to 6-year terms, and there are no term limits.

The Constitution gave senators **staggered terms** (Article I, Section 3). The very first crop of senators were divided into 3 classes: one class had a 2-year term, one class had a 4-year term, and one class had a 6-year term. After the first crop, all senators have had 6-year terms. The result: now, about 1/3 of the senators are up for re-election every 2 years.

The Framers of the Constitution were looking out for us. Six years is a long time to be stuck with the *same* 100 politicians and the same political party controlling the Senate. Staggered terms allow Us The People to "clean house" every couple years.

To be eligible to be a senator, a person must—

- Be at least 30 years old
- Be a U.S. citizen for at least 9 years
- Live in the state he or she represents

Those requirements are in the Constitution (Article I, Section 3).

Senators used to be chosen by each state's legislature. The 17th Amendment changed that. Now, The People of each state directly elect their senators.

All Senate members can vote on bills. The U.S. Vice President—who serves as the Senate President but *isn't* elected to the Senate—can vote only to break ties. The Constitution made that so (Article I, Section 3).

## Congress's Powers

### Legislative Powers

Congress has the power to legislate (make laws)—but about what things? For starters, the things listed in Article 1, Section 8 of the Constitution, which are called the **enumerated powers**. Here are a few examples:

- Power to raise revenue
- Power to coin money
- Power to set up post offices
- Power to establish weights and measures
- Power to declare war

Some enumerated powers were written more clearly than others. The less-clear ones have ignited intense lawsuits.

Why? Because if Congress can regulate certain activities, the states lose some power. Also, it can cost money for states, businesses, or people to comply with federal law.

For example, the U.S. government started heavily regulating air-polluting businesses in the 1970s because some states allowed factories to belch out more pollution than others. Here are some basic arguments:

- **State:** I have rights—the U.S. government is violating those rights by regulating pollution within my borders.

- **Business:** complying with anti-pollution laws costs me money and drives up the price of my products; thus, the U.S. government should stop regulating pollution.

- **U.S. Gov:** pollution ruins the environment and refuses to stay in one state. Not regulating it will give people health problems and cost them money.

The arguments are actually more complex than that. The point is that many people's interests are impacted by the answer to this question: How far do Congress's powers reach?

## House's & Senate's Unique Powers

### Removing Officials from Office

The Constitution gives Congress the power to remove some officials from office through the **impeachment process**, including federal judges, cabinet members, the Vice President, and the President (Article I, Sections 2 & 3 and Article II, Section 4). Members of Congress face a different removal process.

The House has the power to **impeach** officials (accuse them of wrongdoing). The Senate has the power to hold impeachment trials and **convict** officials.

Conviction requires a 2/3 vote of the Senate members present for the vote and removal from office is the only result. Presidential impeachment is covered in Chapter 4.

### Rules for Each Chamber & Enforcement

The House makes its own rules for how it operates, and the Senate makes its own rules (Article I, Section 5). Each chamber's rules cover many issues, including members' conduct, debating, and voting.

The Senate's rules are different from the House's but address many of the same issues. You can find each chamber's rules at its website.

### Power to Confirm Appointments & Treaties

The President has the power to (1) appoint many government officials and (2) make treaties with foreign governments. The Senate has the power to confirm or reject appointments and treaties (Article II, Section 2).

If the President appoints a Vice President because the last one died or left office, the appointment would require House and Senate approval (25th Amendment). Some international agreements, like those dealing with trade, also require House and Senate approval.

## Political Parties & Other Groups

### The Congresses & Party Control

The word "Congress" refers to—

(1)  the legislative body and

(2)  that body during the 2 years between elections.

Congress's membership can change every 2 years because congressional elections happen every 2 years. The Congresses are numbered: the 1st Congress started in 1789 and ended in 1791.

The Republican and Democratic parties aren't mentioned in the Constitution—they didn't exist in the 1700s. Still, they play major roles in Congress.

Below is a list of Congresses from the 105th through the 115th and which party controlled each chamber:

| Congress | Years | House Control | Senate Control |
|---|---|---|---|
| 105th | 1997-99 | Repub. | Repub. |
| 106th | 1999-01 | Repub. | Repub. |
| 107th | 2001-03 | Repub. | Repub. |
| 108th | 2003-05 | Repub. | Repub. |
| 109th | 2005-07 | Repub. | Repub. |
| 110th | 2007-09 | Dem. | Dem. |
| 111th | 2009-11 | Dem. | Dem. |
| 112th | 2011-13 | Repub. | Dem. |
| 113th | 2013-15 | Repub. | Dem. |
| 114th | 2015-17 | Repub. | Repub. |
| 115th | 2017-19 | Repub. | Repub. |

## Caucuses & Other Groups

### In the House

The word **caucus** has a few meanings. Here, it means a group of members of Congress. The House's two largest caucuses are the major-party caucuses:

- The Republican Conference
- The Democratic Caucus

All Republican House Members are members of the Republican Conference. All House Democrats are members of the Democratic Caucus. Typically, independent members "caucus with" (join) one of the major-party caucuses.

The major-party caucuses unite members of the same party so they can more easily accomplish goals. Each major-party caucus chooses its caucus leaders. Usually, the party that controls the House chooses the House's leaders. Details about the major-party caucuses are at **www.dems.gov** and **www.gop.gov**.

The House has informal groups called Congressional Member Organizations or **CMOs**—also confusingly called **caucuses**. CMOs are groups of members who have interests in common or want to get certain things done. There is power in numbers because getting things done usually requires voting.

During the 115th Congress, the House had over 700 CMOs. Here are some examples:

- California Public Higher Education Caucus
- Congressional Black Caucus (race-related)
- Congressional Cannabis Caucus (marijuana)
- Friends of Switzerland Caucus
- House Aerospace Caucus
- Problem Solvers Caucus (for real)

For more about House caucuses, search the House website for "caucus" or "CMO."

### In the Senate

The Senate also has two major-party groups: (1) the majority party and (2) the minority party. These days, the groups call themselves the **Republican Conference** and the **Senate Democrats**. Details are at www.republicans.senate.gov and www.democrats.senate.gov.

Like the House, the Senate has CMOs. Here are a few examples:

- Missile States Coalition
- Senate Chicken Caucus (food, not cowards)

- Senate Human Rights Caucus
- Senate Bipartisan Small Brewers Caucus (beer)

For more about Senate caucuses, search the Senate website for "caucus" or "CMO."

# Leadership Within the Chambers

### The House (Article I, Section 2)

The House can choose (spelled "chuse" back in 1787) its leaders and officers. The House's head honcho is the **Speaker of the House** and is elected by the whole House. The Speaker is usually in the majority party because it has more votes than the minority party.

Among other things, the Speaker presides over the House: calls the House to order, preserves order, lets members speak, and decides whether a member's actions break the rules. The Speaker influences policy by setting the House's agenda and speaking to the national media. The Speaker also plays a role in deciding which members get on which committees (committees are covered later in this chapter).

At the start of each new Congress, each party elects its own leaders. Below are three key leaders and officers from each party in the House (115th Congress: Republicans were the majority):

### Majority Party Leadership (R)

- Majority Party Leader
- Majority Whip
- Republican Conference Chairman

### Minority Party Leadership (D)

- Democratic Leader (Minority Leader)
- Democratic Whip (Minority Whip)
- Democratic Caucus Chairman

Among other things, the **Majority Leader** (with the Speaker) decides which bills the party wants to pass or block. The **Minority Leader** does the same for her or his party and represents the party's members on the House floor.

The **whips** crack whips, so to speak. They pressure party members to vote on certain bills the way the party's leaders want.

The **Republican Conference Chairman** presides over meetings of all Republican House members. The **Democratic Caucus Chairman** organizes all Democrats in the House.

The House website lists all leadership positions and gives details about their functions.

## The Senate (Article I, Section 3)

The Senate can "chuse" its officers, except the **President of the Senate,** who is automatically the U.S. Vice President (Article I, Section 3). The Senate President can't vote in the Senate except to break a tie. The Senate President can't even address the Senate unless the members unanimously say it's okay. Basically, the Senate President presides over the Senate—and not very often.

The Senate elects a **President Pro Tempore** (*pro tempore* means for the time), who presides over the Senate when the Senate President is absent. The President Pro Tempore is an elected member of the Senate, so he or she can vote and address the Senate.

Senate leadership is similar to House leadership. While the House Speaker is the leader of the whole House, the Senate Majority Leader is the leader of the whole Senate. Below are three key leadership positions for each party in the Senate (115th Congress):

### Majority Party Leadership (R)

- Republican Leader (Majority Leader)
- Republican Conference Chairman
- Republican Policy Committee Chairman

### Minority Party Leadership (D)

- Democratic Conference Chairman (Minority Leader)
- Democratic Whip
- Chairman of Policy & Communications Committee

The Senate website lists leadership positions and gives details about their functions.

## Committees

### They Are Very Important

### What They Are

**Committees** are formal groups of House or Senate members that focus on certain issues. Much of Congress's work gets done by committees.

Each chamber's tasks get divvied up among committees. Each committee has **jurisdiction**—authority to deal with certain issues and tasks. The committee structure is complex, and some committees' jurisdictions overlap.

During the 115th Congress, there were 21 House committees. Here are 4 examples:

- Education and Workforce Committee.
- Energy and Commerce Committee.

- Intelligence Committee.

- Science, Space, and Technology Committee.

The Senate has committees, too. To learn more about committees, start at the House or Senate website. If you want to know which committees your members sit on, check those members' webpages for committee assignments.

### Role in Legislative (Lawmaking) Process

Committees are crucial to lawmaking: they decide whether to kill a bill or send it to a full House or Senate vote. They affect what a bill looks like before it goes to a full vote. The legislative process is covered later in this Chapter.

### Role in Congressional Oversight

Congress has a duty to exercise **oversight**: to check on and make sure government agencies are doing what they're supposed to do. Different committees have oversight jurisdiction over different aspects of government.

For example, the Senate Intelligence Committee has jurisdiction over agencies in the "Intelligence Community," like the CIA and Justice Department. The Senate Intel Committee can investigate agencies under its jurisdiction and require them to report to the committee.

Both House and Senate committees have oversight duties. Similar committees in the House and Senate might conduct separate investigations into the same issues at the same time.

### Types of Committees

There are 3 basic types of committees:

- Standing Committees

- Select or Special Committees

- Joint Committees

**Standing** committees continue from one Congress to the next and are permanent because their tasks are ongoing. Examples include the *House Foreign Affairs Committee* and the *Senate Armed Services Committee.*

**Select (or Special)** committees handle special functions that are beyond a standing committee's authority or capacity. Some select committees are temporary. For example, the House established a select committee to investigate the terrorist attacks on U.S. facilities in Benghazi, Libya.

Some select committees are permanent, like the Senate's Select Committee on Ethics. Among other things, that committee can investigate whether a senator violated the Senate's conduct code. The Senate's *Committee on Ethics* is permanent because ethics issues can come up any time.

**Joint committees** have members from the House and the Senate. They handle specific issues or tasks of interest to both chambers. For example, the *Joint Committee on the Library* deals with the Library of Congress, an agency that houses Congress's records.

### Subcommittees and Their Sub-Issues

Many committees cover broad issues that encompass sub-issues. Dividing those committees into **subcommittees** divides a committee's workload and makes it easier to get things done.

For example, the *House Appropriations Committee* deals with **appropriations** (deciding how tax dollars are spent). That's a huge category because Congress appropriates funds for thousands of government functions and agencies—too many for an undivided committee to handle.

The House Appropriations Committee has 12 sub-committees (115th Congress). Here are 3 examples:

- Subcommittee on Commerce, Justice, Science, and Related Agencies.

- Subcommittee on Defense.

- Subcommittee on Labor, Health and Human Services, Education, and Related Agencies.

Many Senate committees also have subcommittees. You can learn about specific subcommittees by starting at a major committee's webpage at the House or Senate website.

## Legislative (Lawmaking) Process

### Basic Overview of Process

**Bills** are proposed laws. Only a member of the House or Senate can introduce bills in that chamber. Members may introduce bills at the request of the President or other people.

Most types of bills may originate in either chamber. **House bills** originate in the House, and **Senate bills** originate in the Senate. Bills are labeled with an abbreviation + a number:

- H.R. 1001 (House bills)

- S. 1001 (Senate bills)

Different bills go through different processes before becoming laws (statutes). Below is a simple illustration of the process for a **House bill that became a law**:

1. House member introduces bill.

2. Bill goes to House committee(s) with jurisdiction over bill's subject(s).

3. Committee votes to send bill for floor vote (vote of whole House).

4. House passes bill by majority vote.

5. Senate passes identical version of bill.

6. President signs bill, and it becomes law.

**It's not usually that simple.** Many things can happen during the basic steps listed above. The next subsection covers some of those things.

## Some Details about the Legislative Process

A bill's journey to become a law can be an intense obstacle course. A bill could die in a committee. A bill could endure so many changes that the passed version looks nothing like the original.

Committees (or subcommittees) are where the obstacles begin. A committee might do any of these things after getting a bill:

- Seek input from agencies affected by the bill.
- Get reports about a bill's likely costs and consequences.
- Hold hearings, where witnesses testify in favor of or against the bill.

Committees usually hold **markup** sessions to debate and maybe change a bill. A lot can happen to a bill during markup if the people involved have clashing agendas.

Eventually, a committee votes on whether to send a bill to the whole chamber for a floor vote. A committee could kill a bill by not voting to send it to the whole chamber.

Things could go wrong even after a committee sends a bill to the whole chamber for a floor vote. Some members might add amendments (changes). Some might try to block the bill from getting to a floor vote. The House and Senate have different rules about debating, amending, and voting on bills.

Even if the first chamber passes a bill and sends it to the other chamber, the bill isn't necessarily in the clear. The second chamber might object to parts of the bill and change it. If so, the new version would go back to the first chamber because a bill can't become law unless both chambers pass identical bills.

If the House and Senate don't agree on a bill, they might set up a Conference Committee: a group of members from each chamber who meet to resolve differences. If the conference committee agrees to one version of a bill, it goes to each chamber for a floor vote.

Once a bill is **enrolled** (passed by both chambers), it is presented to the President, who can do one of 3 things:

(1)   Sign it (bill becomes law).

(2)   Veto it (bill doesn't become law at that point).

(3)   Do nothing (bill might become law).

If the President vetoes the bill, Congress can override the veto by a 2/3 vote of each chamber. Getting that many Members to agree to override a veto is not easy, so overrides are rare.

If the President does nothing with a bill for 10 days after it's presented while Congress is in session, the bill would automatically become law. If the President doesn't sign the bill and Congress goes out of session (recesses) before the 10 days are up, the bill would not become law: that's called a **pocket veto.**

Congress could prevent a pocket veto by not going on recess within 10 days after presenting a bill to the President.

The President's role in the legislative process is in the Constitution (Article I, Section 7). You can find more details about the process by searching online for the terms Congress + legislative process.

## Resolutions: A Form of Legislative Action

Bills are one form of legislative action, and resolutions are another. There are 3 types of resolutions:

(1)   Joint Resolutions

(2)   Concurrent Resolutions

(3)   Simple Resolutions

**Joint resolutions** are like bills: they are binding law and require passage by the House and Senate. Most joint resolutions are presented to the President for approval (like bills are).

Congress often uses joint resolutions for emergency or continuing appropriations. Joint resolutions are the only way Congress can propose amendments to the Constitution. That type of resolution isn't sent to the President because presidents don't have a formal role in amending the Constitution.

**Concurrent resolutions** aren't binding law and aren't sent to the President, but they require passage by the House and Senate. Congress tends to use concurrent resolutions to deal with issues affecting both chambers, like scheduling Congress's adjournment and dealing with rules that apply to both chambers.

Congress also uses concurrent resolutions to express sentiments, like recognizing the anniversary of another nation's independence or condemning the actions of a terrorist group. There aren't many limits on the sentiments that Congress can express through concurrent resolutions.

**Simple resolutions** are passed by only one chamber and aren't binding laws. Each chamber uses simple resolutions to deal with rules and internal affairs or to express that chamber's sentiments.

Like bills, resolutions are labeled and numbered. Those **originating in the House** are labeled with an abbreviation + a number (the numbers below are made up):

- Joint Resolution: H.J. Res. 733
- Concurrent Resolution: H.Con. Res. 55
- Simple Resolution: H. Res. 1001

Resolutions **originating in the Senate** are labeled this way:

- Joint Resolution: S.J. Res. 15
- Concurrent Resolution: S.Con. Res. 52
- Simple Resolution: S. Res. 76

You can find more details about resolutions generally at www.House.gov or www.Senate.gov. You can find resolutions that were voted on at www.Congress.gov.

## Legislative Branch Agencies

Congress has created agencies within the Legislative Branch, which support and work for Congress. Four of the better-known ones are—

- The Congressional Budget Office
- The Government Accountability Office
- The Library of Congress
- The U.S. Capitol Police

The **Congressional Budget Office** (CBO) reports on budget and economic issues. It also estimates how much it would cost the taxpayers if a certain bill is passed. You can find all sorts of budget and spending information at **www.cbo.gov**. The CBO is known for being non-partisan.

The **Government Accountability Office** (GAO) puts out reports on all sorts of policy issues: border security, social security, healthcare, education, etc. You can find GAO reports at **www.gao.gov**. The GAO is known for being non-partisan.

The **Library of Congress** (LOC) is the largest library in the world. It hosts **www.Congress.gov**, where you can track legislation, check how members voted on bills, and find tons of other information. The LOC also houses the Congressional Research Service and the U.S. Copyright office. For more details, visit the LOC online: **www.loc.gov**.

The **Capitol Police** protects Congress, its staff, visitors, and various buildings and grounds. Although the Capitol Police is a law-enforcement agency, it's within the Legislative Branch (not the Executive Branch). Its website is **www.uscp.gov**.

## Washington, D.C.: The Seat of Government

The Framers of the Constitution didn't want the nation's capital to owe anything to or be influenced by any state. That's why the Constitution required Congress to put the seat of government in a district that isn't in a state and to put the district under Congress's jurisdiction (Article I, Section 8). That's Washington, the District of Columbia: aka, "the District" or "D.C."

D.C. has evolved as a city. It has a mayor and a city council, but Congress can override any local law that D.C. passes. The Constitution gives states the right to have representatives in Congress, and D.C. isn't a state, so it doesn't have senators or a full-voting member of the House.

There's a movement to make D.C. a state. We'll see what happens.

## Congress's Pay

Members of Congress get a base salary plus benefits and allowances. The amounts are set **by law**, meaning Congress can give itself raises (Article I, Section 6). The 27th Amendment prevents salary changes from taking effect until the next Congress convenes, meaning the next odd-numbered year.

In 2017, the base yearly salary for most Members was $174,000. Members in leadership positions got more. Members also get an allowance for expenses, which helps cover the high costs of being a Member of Congress. Members maintain a household in their state and one in D.C. They also travel a lot between their state and D.C.

For more details, search the House or Senate website for "salaries" or "compensation."

# Chapter 4

# Executive Branch:
# President & Agencies

**What this Chapter Covers:**

- Presidents Are Not Kings

- Term, Eligibility, & Pay

- Executive Branch: Basic Function & Size

- Presidential Powers, Limits & Duties

- Vice President: A Constitutional Hybrid

- Executive Office of the President (EOP)

- Executive Branch Departments

- The Cabinet

- Independent Agencies

- Presidential Actions

- Electing the President & Vice President

- Removing Presidents or Others from Office

## Presidents Are Not Kings

Next time a presidential candidate promises to lower your income taxes, raise an eyebrow and think "separation of powers." Only Congress has the power to make laws and tax our incomes (Constitution: Article I and 16th Amendment).

Presidents can sign tax-cutting bills passed by Congress. Presidents can try to persuade Congress to lower taxes. But **presidents cannot** single-handedly lower your income taxes—and they can't declare war, create courts, or do anything else reserved for Congress.

Presidents can do some things on their own but not others. That's the nature of **checks and balances**. And that's what our Founding Fathers wanted because they didn't want our government ruled by kings or other dictators.

## Term, Eligibility & Pay

Presidents are elected for **4 years**, but there are term limits (22nd Amendment). The general limit is 2 terms. People who have held the Office of President for more than 2 years (like a vice president who took over for a president who had died) can be elected to only 1 term.

To be eligible to be President, a person must be —

- At least 35 years old
- A natural-born citizen of the U.S.
- A U.S. resident for at least 14 years

The President's yearly salary is $400,000 (2017) and stays the same during the term the President was elected for. The salary is set by law, which requires Congress's action (U.S. Code, Title 3). Presidents also have expense accounts and benefits, including the right to live in the White House.

# Executive Branch: Basic Functions & Size

Congress makes policies, mainly by passing laws. Policies are only ideas until someone **executes** them (puts them into effect). Executing the law is one function of the Executive Branch.

Let's say that Congress passes a law to help certain types of small businesses by giving them loans. Congress creates a money pot worth $500 million to fund the loans.

The money wouldn't magically flow into those businesses' accounts. Someone has to set up a process for businesses to apply for the loans. Someone has to make sure that only businesses that meet Congress's criteria get the money. Someone has to send checks or arrange electronic deposits. Those kinds of practicalities are what executing the law is about.

**Enforcing** laws is another Executive Branch function. For example, federal law prohibits people from possessing certain drugs. Enforcing drug laws requires people to investigate and prosecute people who break the drug laws. The Executive Branch handles those things.

The Executive Branch must execute and enforce huge numbers of laws, which requires a lot of people. Not counting members of the armed services, more than 2 million people work for the Executive Branch.

Some Executive Branch agencies have offices throughout the nation. For example, the FBI has over 50 field offices that handle investigations throughout the U.S. The State Department has over 25 regional offices handling passports in the U.S. and also has embassies in many foreign countries.

## Presidential Powers, Limits & Duties

### Powers Granted by Constitution

Among other things, Article II of the Constitution grants the President the power to—

- Command the military
- Pardon people convicted of crimes
- Make treaties with other nations
- Appoint many government officials

The Constitution also limits the President's powers. For example, the President is the Commander in Chief (military), but only Congress can declare war. The President appoints judges but needs the Senate's approval. The President makes treaties with other nations but needs the Senate's approval.

### Authority Granted by Congress

The Constitution gives Congress the power to delegate authority to the Executive Branch. That makes sense because Congress relies on the Executive Branch to execute and enforce laws.

Congress can create an Executive Branch agency or change an existing agency. After the 9/11 attacks, Congress created the Department of Homeland Security through statutes. Congress dictated some details and left others to the Executive Branch. For example, Congress stated the department's primary mission and laid out official positions at the top, like *Secretary* and *Deputy Secretary*.

Senate approval is required for certain presidential appointments, but Congress can give the President authority to appoint lower officers without Senate approval (Article II, Section 2).

Congress can also give an Executive Branch agency **rulemaking power**: the power to make regulations. The basic idea is that

Congress sets the broader policies through statutes and gives an executive agency the authority to handle some details and logistics through regulations.

Agencies' regulations and procedures are what **Administrative Law** is about, and it is complex. Congress laid out procedures and standards regarding administrative law in the Administrative Procedures Act and other statutes (U.S. Code, Title 5).

### Some Duties & Limits

The Constitution gives presidents the **duty** to "take care that the laws be faithfully executed" (Article II, Section 3). This means that presidents must execute and enforce even laws they don't like.

Specific presidential duties covered in Article II include—

- Informing Congress of the state of the union.
- Commissioning officers of the U.S.
- Receiving ambassadors from other nations.

Statutes also create duties for the President, like those relating to the federal budget. For example, the Constitution says very little about the President's role in the budget, but Congress has passed statutes affecting the President's role in the budget process.

Congress can impose duties and limits on presidents, as long as Congress doesn't overstep its constitutional authority. One **check** against Congress treating the President like a mindless puppet is the President's veto power. But there's a **counter-check**: Congress can override a veto.

## Vice President: A Constitutional Hybrid

The Constitution gives the Vice President a role in the Executive and Legislative Branches (Articles I and II). Thus, vice presidents are hybrids, like cars that run on both gas and electricity.

**In the Executive Branch**, the Vice President's main function is to take over if the President dies, resigns, or can't fulfill the duties of office for other reasons. The Constitution doesn't give vice presidents a detailed job description.

That's why different vice presidents do the job differently. Vice presidents often handle ceremonial duties, like going to funerals or meeting with heads of other nations. Some vice presidents publicly promote the President's policies.

Congress can assign duties to vice presidents. For example, Congress put the Vice President on the National Security Council back in the 1940s, and the Vice President is still on it today.

**In the Legislative Branch**, the Vice President automatically serves as the President of the Senate (Chapter 3). The Vice President doesn't vote in the Senate—except to break a tie—and doesn't usually preside over the Senate unless a vote requires a tie breaker.

Vice presidents have their own offices and staff. The Vice President's official residence is a mansion at the Naval Observatory in Washington, D.C. The White House website (www.whitehouse.gov) has more details about the Vice President.

## Executive Office of the President (EOP)

Presidents oversee a lot of activities and need a lot of staff, which is part of the Executive Office of the President (EOP). In 2017, more than 1,800 people worked for the EOP, and its budget was more than $700 million.

The **White House Chief of Staff** oversees the EOP. The EOP houses various offices, including those listed below.

### Examples: Offices Within the EOP

- Council of Economic Advisers

- Office of National Security Advisor

- Office of the Vice President

- Office of Management and Budget

- Office of the U.S. Trade Representative

The President can appoint many high-level staffers **without the Senate's approval**, like the White House Chief of Staff. Some positions require Senate approval, like the Director of the Office of Management and Budget.

The EOP has multiple levels of staff, like Assistant to the President, Deputy Assistant, and Special Assistant. One of the most visible staffers is the Press Secretary, who speaks to the public for the President.

Some staffers work in the White House building. Most work in the Eisenhower Executive Office Building (EEOB), a building near the White House that's worth photographing. For more about the EOP, search the White House website.

## Executive Branch Departments

Departments are the largest units of the Executive Branch. There are 15 departments that help execute and enforce our laws. Congress can create new departments or change existing ones.

Most executive agencies fall under a department. Each department handles different policy issues. A list of departments is below, and their names give some idea of what they handle.

### Departments & Their Websites

- **Agriculture** (usda.gov)

- **Commerce** (commerce.gov)

- **Defense** (defense.gov)

- **Education** (ed.gov)

- **Energy** (energy.gov)

- **Health & Human Services** (hhs.gov)

- **Homeland Security** (dhs.gov)

- **Housing & Urban Development** (hud.gov)

- **Interior** (doi.gov)

- **Justice** (justice.gov)

- **Labor** (dol.gov)

- **State** (state.gov)

- **Transportation** (transportation.gov)

- **Treasury** (treasury.gov)

- **Veterans Affairs** (va.gov)

The departments deal with broad issues. For example, the **Department of State** (aka, "State Department") handles issues relating to foreign nations, including sub-issues like diplomatic efforts and passports. The **Secretary of State** heads the State Department and has layers of lower officers plus staff.

Each department is organized differently. For example, the **Justice Department** (whose primary mission is law enforcement) has more than 50 sub-units handling sub-issues. A few examples are below:

- Bureau of Alcohol, Tobacco, & Firearms (ATF)
- Drug Enforcement Administration (DEA)
- Federal Bureau of Investigation (FBI)

- Office of Privacy & Civil Liberties
- Tax Division

Details about what each department does and how it's organized are at each department's website.

Most department heads have the title **Secretary**, like the Secretary of Agriculture. The head of the Justice Department has the title **Attorney General**.

Presidents appoint department heads with Senate approval. The President might appoint department heads based on expertise or for other reasons, like political favors or friendship. The Senate can block unwise appointments but doesn't always do that.

Department heads serve at the President's pleasure and can be fired. Also, Congress can remove department heads from office through the impeachment process.

Departments tend to be big. Below are examples of 4 departments and their approximate number of employees (2017).

| Department | Employees |
|---|---|
| Agriculture | 100,000 |
| Commerce | 38,000 |
| Education | 4,200 |
| Veterans Affairs | 235,000 |

The President has some power to restructure the Executive Branch, but that power is limited by law (U.S. Code, Title 5).

## The Cabinet

The President's **Cabinet** is a group of senior officials who advise the President about issues relating to those officials' positions.

Because Cabinet members have the President's ear, they may have influence over presidential policies.

Historically, the department heads and the Vice President were the Cabinet members. But the President can somewhat reorganize the Cabinet. For example, Presidents Obama and Trump elevated some senior officials to the Cabinet whose positions were not part of the Cabinet before.

Cabinet members can play a part in removing a president from office based on an inability to handle the duties of office, as opposed to bad conduct. Congress has the final say over whether a president is removed from office (more about that later in this chapter).

## Independent Agencies

**"Independent agency"** refers to a commission, board, or other agency that is in the Executive Branch but isn't under a department and isn't under the President's direct control. Here are a few examples:

- Federal Election Commission (FEC)
- National Labor Relations Board (NLRB)
- National Aeronautics & Space Administration (NASA)

Congress creates independent agencies through statutes. The purpose of making an agency independent is to reduce the influence of politics by reducing the President's control.

In many independent agencies, the decision making is done by a group, not one person. For example, Congress gave the Federal Election Commission (FEC) 6 members and required that no more than 3 members be of the same political party. The President appoints FEC commissioners with Senate approval. Commissioners serve 6-year terms, so they could outlast the President who appointed them.

FEC commissioners serve staggered terms, so two seats are open every two years. That structure prevents one president from packing the FEC with partisan cronies.

Independent status doesn't guarantee that agencies will be free from political influences—not by a long shot. It depends on the ethics of the individuals who head an agency.

Typically, the President can fire the heads of independent agencies **for cause**, meaning if they failed to do the job or did something else wrong. It depends on what the relevant statutes say.

# Presidential Actions

### Executive Orders

Executive orders give instructions to Executive Branch agencies about what they should do and what their priorities should be. In 2017, for example, the President signed an executive order instructing agencies to buy American-made goods when possible.

Executive orders are binding (must be followed) if they don't violate the law. Separation of Powers limits what presidents can do through executive orders. For example, a president can't validly issue an executive order that appropriates more money to the Department of Education because presidents don't have the power to appropriate funds; Congress does.

For the most part, the President can issue executive orders that change or revoke past presidents' executive orders. Courts have the power to determine whether executive orders are lawful.

Executive orders are numbered. President Obama's last executive order was numbered EO 13764, and President Trump's first was EO 13765.

Presidents can issue executive orders on their own, without Congress's approval. Executive orders must be published at the

Federal Register (www.federalregister.gov). Some presidents also publish executive orders at the White House website.

## Memoranda (Plural of "Memorandum")

Like executive orders, presidential memoranda instruct executive agencies. In 2017, for example, the President issued a memorandum instructing agency heads to freeze the hiring of non-military employees in the Executive Branch.

The major difference between executive orders and memoranda is that orders have to be published in the Federal Register but memoranda don't. Some presidents make memoranda publicly available, anyway.

Because memoranda don't have to be published, presidents typically use them for routine actions that the public isn't interested in, like managing staff. You can check for presidential memoranda at the White House website, but not all memoranda are necessarily published there.

## Proclamations

Presidential **proclamations** are statements, things that presidents proclaim. There are no constitutional requirements, so proclamations can address all sorts of things.

One of the most famous is the Emancipation Proclamation, issued by Abe Lincoln, which was one step in the process of freeing slaves. The National Archives has details (www.archives.gov).

In modern times, proclamations are often used in a ceremonial way, like recognizing a person or issue. For example, a proclamation proclaimed one day to be Military Spouse Day.

Some presidents use proclamations to issue pardons to people convicted of crimes. Presidents have also used proclamations to address trade or foreign affairs issues.

While executive orders have the force of law, proclamations don't unless authorized by Congress. Proclamations are published in the Federal Register. Some presidents also publish proclamations at the White House website.

# Electing the President & Vice President

### Political Parties & Ballot Access

Political parties play a huge role in electing presidents. The 2 major (dominant) parties are the Democrats and the Republicans. **Third-party candidates** are from other parties. **Independent candidates** aren't part of a formal party—confusing because there is a party called the "American Independent Party."

Each major party has a **national-level organization**: the Republican National Committee (RNC) and the Democratic National Committee (DNC). The major parties also have **state-level organizations**, like the North Dakota Republican Party and the Wyoming Democrats. The same is true of some smaller parties, like the Libertarian and Green parties.

**Ballot access** refers to candidates' ability to get on a state's general-election ballot so people can easily vote for them. State and federal laws affect candidates' ballot access.

In the 2016 election, the presidential candidates of only 3 parties made it onto all 50 states' ballots: Democrat, Republican, and Libertarian. The Green Party candidate was on the ballot in 44 states and Washington, D.C., and she qualified to have her name written in by voters in 3 states.

Third-party candidates tend to get fewer votes. Here's the Election 2016 vote count (from www.fec.gov):

- Democrat (Clinton): 65,853,516
- Republican (Trump): 62,984,825

- Libertarian (Johnson): 4,489,221
- Green (Stein): 1,457,216

Third-party candidates can have significant effects on elections. First, they get media attention and can influence public opinion. Second, they sometimes draw votes away from major-party candidates.

For example, some people who voted for Gary Johnson might have voted for Donald Trump instead if Johnson had not run. The same can be said about Jill Stein and Hillary Clinton. We can't know how many votes a third-party candidate took away from a major candidate because we don't know how many voters would have refused to vote for a major candidate if the third-party candidate hadn't run.

## Basic Overview of the Electoral Process

We The People directly elect members of Congress—one person, one vote. It *seems* like we directly elect presidents and vice presidents because the candidates' names are on the ballots, **but we don't.**

By voting for a "ticket" (the presidential and vice-presidential candidates who run for office as a team), we're actually voting for a group of "electors" (people) in our state whom we want to vote for our candidates through the Electoral College, which meets more than a month after Election Day.

It sounds weird because it is (more about the Electoral College in the next subsection).

Here are the basic steps in the electoral process:

- Political parties hold state primaries or caucuses.
- Political parties hold national nominating conventions.
- The People vote in the General Election (November).
- The Electoral College votes (December).
- Congress counts the Electoral College votes.

The next few subsections are in reverse order, starting with the general election and working backward to the primaries and caucuses.

## General Election

### Election Day

Election Day for presidents happens every 4 years on the Tuesday after the first Monday in November. That date is set by statute (U.S. Code, Title 3).

### Electoral College

The **Electoral College** isn't a place. It's a process involving a group of people who vote to elect a president and vice president.

The Electoral College has 538 **electors**, people from the states and Washington, D.C. Each state political party chooses its own "slate" (group) of electors. The electors are supposed to vote for that party's presidential and vice-presidential candidates if those candidates win the state's general election. Party rules and state law affect the process for choosing a state's electors for the Electoral College.

Why 538 electors? Each state gets the same number of electors as the number of members the state has in Congress. In 2016, for example, Virginia had 11 House members and 2 senators: thus, 13 electors in the Electoral College.

There are **535** state electors: the same number as all voting members of Congress. The 23rd Amendment (1961) gave Washington D.C. some Electoral College votes. In 2016, D.C. had **3** electoral votes: **535 + 3 = 538.**

On Election Day, The People in each state vote for a presidential candidate's "ticket," which includes that candidate's running mate (person running for vice president).

Most states have a **winner-takes-all** system: the candidate who wins the most votes in a state wins all electoral votes in that state. Some states have a **winner-takes-most** system.

In the December after Election Day, the Electoral College "meets." The 538 electors don't gather in one place like a huge cocktail party. Instead, electors go to their state capitol to cast their votes for president (and vice president). The candidate who gets at least **270 electoral votes** (more than half of 538) wins the Presidency.

Why such a complex system for electing presidents? Because the Founding Fathers disagreed about how to elect a president. Some wanted The People to directly elect presidents, some wanted Congress to do it, and some wanted the states to do it. The Electoral College was a compromise (Article II, Section 1 and 12th Amendment).

### Popular Vote Versus Electoral Votes

The **popular vote** is the number of votes cast by The People. More than 130 million people voted in the 2016 presidential election.

**Electoral votes** are those cast by the 538 members of the Electoral College. Usually, the candidate who wins the popular vote also wins the electoral votes. So far, only 5 presidents have **lost the popular vote**:

- John Quincy Adams (1824)
- Rutherford Hayes (1876)
- Benjamin Harrison (1888)
- George W. Bush (2000)
- Donald Trump (2016)

## The Parties' National Conventions

The major parties and some smaller parties each hold a national convention to choose the party's nominee for president. Below are the 4 better-known parties' nominees for Election 2016:

- Republican Party: Donald Trump
- Democratic Party: Hillary Clinton
- Green Party: Jill Stein
- Libertarian Party: Gary Johnson

For the 2 major parties, each state-level party chooses **delegates** (party members) to attend the national party's convention and vote for a certain candidate to become the nominee. Each party has its own rules for choosing the nominee.

## Primaries & Caucuses

**Primaries** are public elections, run by state and local governments. In a state primary, the voters choose which candidate they want the state party's delegates to vote for at the national convention. The states choose when to hold their primaries.

**Caucuses** have the same purpose as primaries: choosing a state party's pick for presidential nominee. While primaries are publicly run elections, caucuses are privately run by political parties' insiders. Usually, people at caucuses openly debate and vote for candidates they want to become the party's nominee.

State-level parties decide whether to have primaries or caucuses. In 2016, for example, the Republican and Democratic parties of Iowa each held caucuses. In Kentucky, the Republicans held caucuses, and Democrats held a primary.

The systems and rules for choosing a party's nominee for president can be complex and weird. The best way to learn about how your state-level party handles it is to visit the party's website.

# Removing Presidents or Others from Office

## Impeachment Process: Wrongdoing

Impeachment is about crimes or other wrongdoing. The Constitution says that presidents and other "civil officers" can be removed from office if impeached and convicted of "Treason, Bribery, or other high Crimes and Misdemeanors" (Article II, Section 4). The Constitution doesn't say what qualifies as "high crimes and misdemeanors."

In this context, **impeach** means to bring charges that accuse someone of wrongdoing. Impeachment is only one step in the process of removing a president from office.

**Articles of Impeachment** contain the written charge(s) against a president. The Constitution gives the House the power to impeach (Article I, Section 2). The House can impeach a president by adopting Articles of Impeachment through a majority vote.

If a president is impeached, the Senate holds an **impeachment trial**. It takes a 2/3 vote of the Senate to **convict** a president (find him or her guilty). If convicted, a president is removed from office.

Only 2 presidents have been impeached. The House impeached Andrew Johnson in 1868 partly because he had removed an official from office without Congress's approval. The Senate **acquitted** (didn't convict) Johnson, so he stayed in office.

The House impeached Bill Clinton in 1998. The charges related to his false testimony about a sexual affair he'd had with a woman. The Senate acquitted Clinton.

Richard Nixon was on the road to impeachment over the Watergate cover-up. The proceedings began in 1974, but Nixon resigned before the process was complete.

## The 25th Amendment: Removing Presidents

### Death, Resignation, or Removal

The 25th Amendment covers what happens if a president dies in office, resigns, or is removed (by impeachment or another way). On a president's death, resignation, or removal, the Vice President takes over as Acting President.

### Presidents Removing Themselves

Presidents can resign from office, like Richard Nixon did. Resignation is permanent.

The 25th Amendment gives presidents a way to **temporarily remove themselves** from office if they're "unable to discharge the powers and duties" of office. For example, George W. Bush temporarily transferred his power to his Vice President before going under anesthesia for surgery.

To remove himself or herself, the President must send to the House Speaker and the Senate President Pro Tempore **a letter** declaring that the President is unable to discharge the powers and duties of office. Then the Vice President takes over as Acting President.

To reclaim the powers, the President must send to the same people a letter stating that the President is again able to handle the powers and duties.

### Other People Removing Presidents

The 25th Amendment gives a special group of officials a way to remove a president who isn't able "to discharge the powers and duties of office." To do that, the Vice President plus "a majority of either the principal officers of the executive departments or of such other body as Congress may by law provide" must send to the House and Senate leaders a letter stating that the President is unable to handle the duties of office. Then the Vice President takes over as Acting President.

It's not clear whether the special group that can send the removal letter is the Vice President plus only the 15 department heads or plus the President's full Cabinet (some presidents have included people in the Cabinet who were not department heads).

After the special group sends a removal letter to the House and Senate leaders, the President could take over again by sending to the same people a letter stating that the President is able again. If nobody prevents it, the President would go back to work.

But it could go differently. The Vice President and a majority of the special group could send to the House and Senate leaders another letter stating the President really isn't able to handle the powers and duties.

If that happens, Congress could decide—by a 2/3 vote of each chamber—that the president isn't able. In that case, the President would be out, and the Vice President would stay on as Acting President. But if Congress doesn't vote within a certain amount of time to remove the President, the President would continue in office.

### Order of Succession: Who Takes Over

The Vice President is the first in line to take over if the President dies, resigns, or is removed from office. But what if the Vice President isn't able to serve when the President dies or leaves office?

That's what the **order of succession** is about, also called "line of succession." It covers which officials would step in and in what order. The order is—

1. Vice President

2. Speaker of the House

3. Senate President Pro Tempore

4. Secretary of State

5. Secretary of the Treasury

6.  Secretary of Defense

7.  Attorney General

8.  Secretary of the Interior

9.  Secretary of Agriculture

10. Secretary of Commerce

11. Secretary of Labor

12. Secretary of Health and Human Services

13. Secretary of Housing and Urban Development

14. Secretary of Transportation

15. Secretary of Energy

16. Secretary of Education

17. Secretary of Veterans Affairs

18. Secretary of Homeland Security

Let's say that a president and vice president died or became incapacitated at the same time. In that case, the Speaker of the House would step in.

What if the Speaker couldn't take over for some reason? In that case, the Senate's President Pro Tempore would step in. And so on.

The order of succession is set by statute (Title 3, U.S. Code, Section 19). Thus, the order can change if Congress wants to change it.

# Chapter 5

# Judicial Branch:
# Courts & Agencies

## What this Chapter Covers:

- Roles & Functions

- Sources of Judicial Branch's Power

- Basics About Court Systems

- Judges: Independence, Terms, & Pay

- Courts' Effect on Law & Public Policy

- Precedents & Stare Decisis

- District Courts (Trial Courts)

- Circuit Courts of Appeal (Appellate Courts)

- The Supreme Court

- Specialty Courts & Judges

- Administrative Law Judges

- Judicial Branch Agencies

## Roles & Functions

### Checks & Balances

The Judicial Branch has the power of **judicial review**, meaning courts can—

- Interpret the Constitution and other laws.
- Decide whether laws are unconstitutional.
- Decide whether government action is illegal.

How a court interprets the law affects your rights and the government's powers. For example, the Constitution protects your freedom of speech against government censoring but doesn't say what "speech" means.

Does it include words you wrote online? Words on a T-shirt? Artwork? How courts have interpreted the word "speech" in the 1st Amendment determines which types of expressions a government can regulate. For example, some artworks involving sexuality (like films or paintings) get 1st Amendment protection, but child pornography does not.

Courts don't have the power to make public policy (Congress does that by passing laws). But courts' interpretations of laws affect public policy—it's unavoidable.

As long as Congress passes any unclear laws, courts will have to interpret some of them. It's part of our courts' duties. And people will continue debating and getting upset over how courts interpret laws.

As well as reviewing laws, courts can review government actions. For example, a court might find that an FBI's raid on a suspect's home was illegal. A court might find that the Veterans Administration's cutting off someone's benefits violated a statute, a regulation, or the Constitution.

Those are a few ways the Judicial Branch acts as a check on the other branches, but checks and balances work in different directions. For example, Congress checks the Judicial Branch through the power to remove judges from the courts.

### Enforcing the Law & Resolving Disputes

The Executive Branch enforces the law, and the Judicial Branch plays a role. That's true in criminal and civil cases. **Criminal cases** involve offenses against the government: actions a government decided to prohibit. Governments, not individuals, prosecute criminal cases. A criminal **defendant** is one who is prosecuted for committing a crime.

Let's say that Darla the Drug Dealer sells illegal drugs online to people in several states. The Executive Branch investigates and prosecutes Darla. If the case goes to trial, it would happen in court (Judicial Branch). The court might convict Darla and impose a sentence, like jail time. The Executive Branch would make sure Darla served the sentence.

**Civil cases** don't involve criminal sentences but do involve laws or legal duties that need to be enforced. For example, if a person has a legal duty to drive a car carefully, the law might require someone who causes an accident to provide a **remedy**, like paying the injured party's medical bills.

Courts are like referees, but courts don't watch the world from the sidelines and step in when they see injustice. To get a court involved in a situation, a party must bring a case to court.

The **parties** in a court case are the people (or entities) that sue or are sued. Almost anyone can be a party in a civil case. For example, you might sue a blogger for publishing things about you that were nasty and false. A business might sue another business for failing to keep a promise in a contract.

In a civil case, the court would resolve the dispute by deciding—based on the law—who was right, who was wrong, and what should happen. For example, a court might order the nasty blogger to compensate you by paying you money.

There are rules for criminal and civil trials, like the rules controlling which evidence is allowed at trial. Part of a court's job is to make sure that the rules are followed at trial.

## Sources of Judicial Branch's Power

The Constitution established only one court: the U.S. Supreme Court (Article III, Section 1). The Constitution also laid out some of the Supreme Court's **jurisdiction**—legal ability to hear cases. If a court doesn't have jurisdiction over a case, the court can't hear that case. Congress has the power to affect some aspects of the Supreme Court's jurisdiction.

Congress also has the power to establish "inferior courts" (Articles I, III, and IV). Congress created the earliest form of our court system through the Judiciary Act of 1789. Other statutes have changed the system over the past 200+ years. The next few sections cover basics about court systems and specific federal courts.

## Basics About Court Systems

### Federal Court System

**Full judicial power** includes the ability to decide cases in which someone's life, liberty, or property is at stake. Not all federal courts have full judicial power.

The main U.S. courts that have full judicial power are—

- The Supreme Court
- Circuit Courts of Appeal
- District Courts

The **district courts** (trial courts) hold trials. In trials, a judge or a jury decides whether someone is guilty in a criminal case or liable in a civil case.

The **circuit courts of appeal** (appellate courts) are higher up the chain. They hear appeals on cases from lower courts and tribunals.

As the highest court, the **Supreme Court** has the last word about a particular case or law. Lower courts must follow Supreme Court decisions. The Supreme Court can review cases from the circuit courts of appeal but also serves other functions.

Types of federal courts are covered in more detail later in this chapter. Also, the federal court system's main website has information about courts, cases, and history (www.uscourts.gov).

## State Court Systems

As well as their own laws, the states have their own court systems, but the courts are named and organized differently. In New York and Maryland, for example, the highest court is the "Court of Appeals." In most states, the highest court is called "Supreme Court," like the Utah Supreme Court

Florida has two levels of trial courts: curcuit courts and county courts. Texas has more trial courts, including district courts, county courts, magistrate courts, and municipal courts.

State court systems are separate from the federal court system, but state and federal courts are interrelated. A state's highest court has the final word about interpretation of state law. The U.S. Supreme court can overrule a state court's interpretation of the U.S. Constitution or other federal law.

## Judges: Independence, Terms, & Pay

The Framers of the Constitution wanted to create an **independent judiciary**—they didn't want courts to be vulnerable to politicians' or other people's influence. Independence promotes fairness, justice, and the Rule of Law.

At least 2 constitutional requirements help promote judges' independence:

- Life appointments
- Salary protection

The main types of federal judges are appointed for life during good behavior. They can stay on the bench until they resign, die, or are removed for bad behavior.

Because of life appointments, judges can outlast elected politicians. If judges were elected instead of appointed, they might feel pressured to decide cases based on politicians' or voters' agendas.

Because a judge's salary can't be reduced after the judge takes office, politicians can't use personal income to pressure judges to decide cases in certain ways.

The President appoints many federal judges, in some cases with Senate approval. The Constitution and some statutes cover the appointment process for different types of judges.

Federal judges can be removed from office through impeachment. If the House impeaches and the Senate convicts a judge, the judge would be out of a job.

Over the past 200+ years, 15 judges were impeached and only 8 were convicted. Here are a few examples of things that got judges removed from the bench:

- Being drunk in court
- Tax evasion

- Perjury (lying under oath)
- Receiving a bribe

That info is from the Federal Judicial Center (www.fjc.gov).

Congress sets federal judges' salaries, which vary based on which court the judge sits on and whether the judge has an administrative position. Federal judges' salaries automatically increase a little each year due to cost-of-living adjustments. The federal courts website has salary data going back about 50 years (www.uscourts.gov).

## Courts' Effect on Law & Public Policy

### Legal Decisions & Political Consequences

Congress and the President make political decisions (those involving public policy). But courts' rulings can have political consequences.

Public policy involves choices about whose interests to protect. Often, the following parties' interests clash:

- Government vs. people
- Government vs. businesses
- People vs. businesses
- Wealthy people vs. poor people

The outcomes of some court cases affect whether the law protects one of those parties' interests more than another's.

In theory, a judge's political ideology should not influence a court's decisions. In reality, some judges' rulings consistently favor certain interests over others. For example, some judges consistently rule to protect ordinary people's rights against government power. Other judges tend to favor governments or big businesses.

### Labels: Conservative, Liberal, Moderate, Activist

Some people label judges and courts based on how they tend to rule. The labels aren't fully reliable, but many media and politicians use them as shorthand anyway.

So-called **conservative** judges are those who tend to protect government's power or big businesses' interests over ordinary people's. So-called **liberal** judges tend to favor people's interests over government's power or big businesses' interests.

**Moderate** is a harder label to pin down. It seems to mean hard to predict.

**Activist** is another iffy label. It refers to judges seen as actively trying to affect public policy through court cases. Judges of all ideologies have, at times, behaved like "activists." Usually, people hurl the word "activist" at a judge if they don't like the effect of that judge's ruling.

## Precedents & Stare Decisis

A **precedent** is a rule or principle stated in a past court case. Consider two voting-rights cases as examples. In *Breedlove v. Suttle* (1937), the U.S. Supreme Court interpreted the Constitution to allow states to require people to pay a poll tax before they could vote in elections for state and local officials.

Poll taxes made it hard for many people to vote. At the time of the *Breedlove* case, America was still in the Great Depression. Many people had to choose between spending money to vote or to buy food.

The 24th Amendment (1964) abolished poll taxes for federal elections, but the *Breedlove* precedent allowed states to charge poll taxes for state elections. In *Harper v. Virginia State Board of Elections* (1966), the Supreme Court reversed the *Breedlove* case and set a new precedent—poll taxes, in all elections, are unconstitutional.

**Stare Decisis** is a principle that compels courts to follow their own precedents: to rule the same way today as they did in similar past cases. Sometimes, courts break their own precedents, as the Supreme Court did with *Breedlove.*

Lower courts must follow the precedents of higher courts within the jurisdiction. Precedents can change, but lower courts can't change a higher court's precedents.

Stare Decisis promotes fairness by increasing the chances that the law is enforced similarly for all people. By following precedents, Courts protect the Rule of Law.

## District Courts (Trial Courts)

### What District Courts Do

Among other things, district courts hold trials to resolve disputes among parties. Whether criminal or civil cases, trial courts determine—

- What happened (the "facts" or "truth")
- Whether a party violated a law or legal duty
- What the law requires the parties to do

At trial, both parties usually argue that the facts (truth), the law, or both are on their side. The parties typically present **evidence** to prove their case, like witness testimony.

Sometimes, a law's validity is challenged at trial. District courts have the power to decide whether a law is constitutional. District courts also have the power to issue orders. A **court order** directs someone to do something or not do something. Here are a few examples of what courts do through orders:

- Set trial dates
- Impose sentences (criminal cases)

- Restrain a person from going near someone
- Require a person to do something

Courts have the power to hold people in **contempt of court** for not following court orders. For example, a court might impose a fine or send someone to jail for disobeying a court order.

## Trials & Your Rights

### Jury Trials

In a jury trial, jurors decide **questions of fact**—which party's version of the "facts" is true. Did a defendant rob a bank? Did a defendant manufacture a dangerous product?

Judges decide **questions of law**, like whether the search of a suspect's house was legal or whether certain evidence should be admitted at trial. Judges also instruct the jury about the law that applies in a case. Here's what usually happens at a jury trial:

- The parties argue their cases, usually through lawyers.
- The judge instructs the jury.
- The jury deliberates (considers evidence). The jury renders a verdict (states the decision).

In a criminal case, the judge usually decides the sentence based on sentencing laws. In a civil case where a party seeks **damages** (money paid for harm suffered), the jury usually decides the amount of damages.

Judges can set aside (invalidate) a jury's verdict in some circumstances, but it doesn't happen often. In criminal cases, judges can set aside a guilty verdict but not a not-guilty verdict.

### Bench Trials

In a **bench trial**, there is no jury. The judge decides questions of both fact and law. The judge decides the outcome of the case.

Some parties prefer a judge over a jury. In complex civil cases, for example, the parties might think a judge will better understand the evidence. In a criminal case, a defendant might prefer a judge and feel that a jury would be biased due to pre-trial media coverage.

## Constitutional Rights Regarding Trials

The Constitution's 5th, 6th, and 8th Amendments address some of our rights regarding criminal cases. The 7th Amendment covers civil trials.

Among other things, the **5th Amendment** protects you against—

- Being punished twice for the same crime
- Being forced to testify against yourself (criminal)
- Being deprived of life, liberty or property without due process of law

The Constitution doesn't say what "due process of law" means. Congress, the Executive Branch, and the courts have played roles in laying out which legal processes must be followed before a government deprives a person of rights or freedoms.

The **6th Amendment** gives criminal defendants the right to a jury trial in all criminal actions. Courts have interpreted that right as not applying to petty crimes, like some traffic laws. The 6th Amendment also gives criminal defendants the right—

- To be informed of the nature of the charges
- To confront witnesses against the defendant
- To compel witnesses to testify (subpoena)
- To have assistance of counsel (a lawyer)
- To a speedy, public trial

The Constitution doesn't say what "speedy" means. It also says nothing about the quality of "assistance of counsel." Must the lawyer have certain skills? What about a lawyer who slams vodka shots before trial? If you're curious about how some courts have ruled on the right to counsel, search online for "ineffective assistance of counsel."

The **8th Amendment** prohibits—

- Excessive fines
- Cruel and unusual punishment
- Excessive bail

The Constitution doesn't say what "excessive" and "cruel and unusual" mean, so courts have had to interpret those terms.

The **7th Amendment** gives people the right to a jury trial in certain types of civil cases. Parties can waive their jury-trial rights and choose a bench trial.

## Types & Appointment of Judges in District Courts

The Constitution gives full **district court judges** life appointments during good behavior. Presidents appoint district judges with Senate approval.

Federal **magistrate judges** work in district courts and help with the workload. Magistrates perform tasks delegated by the courts, as allowed by law.

Bankruptcy courts are special units within district courts. **Bankruptcy judges** work for district courts and hear bankruptcy cases. Congress decides how many bankruptcy judges are in each district.

Magistrate and bankruptcy judges don't have life appointments or salary protection. They are appointed for limited terms by courts, not the President.

## Number, Location & Jurisdiction

There are 94 federal district courts (2017). Every state and certain U.S. territories, like Puerto Rico, have at least one.

Congress divided some states into geographical districts. For example, Georgia has 3 federal judicial districts: Northern, Middle, and Southern. Some smaller states and territories constitute one district, like the District of Delaware and the District of the Virgin Islands.

The Constitution gives Congress the power to set district courts' jurisdiction. Below are 3 examples of the types of cases district courts have jurisdiction over:

- Cases involving the U.S. Constitution or statutes
- Cases involving patents or copyrights
- Certain cases involving citizens of different states.

The U.S. Code covers district courts' jurisdiction (Title 28, Part IV).

Geography plays a part in jurisdiction. If someone commits a federal crime in Gainesville, Florida, the case would likely be tried in the U.S. District Court for the Northern District of Florida because Gainesville is within the Northern District.

## Circuit Courts of Appeals (Appellate Courts)

### What the Circuit Courts Do and Don't Do

Mainly, a federal circuit court of appeals reviews decisions of lower courts and other tribunals located in the circuit. The circuit courts—

- Don't re-try cases
- Don't review new evidence
- Don't have witnesses or juries

Circuit courts usually decide whether legal errors occurred at the trial level, like whether the lower court conducted the proceedings improperly or applied the law incorrectly.

If a lower court made an error, the circuit court could send the case back for the error to be corrected. In some situations, circuit courts have ordered new trials.

Appellate courts don't go around looking for cases. To have a case heard on appeal, a party must petition an appellate court.

## Trials Versus Appeals

At trial, the lawyers on each side take turns arguing their case in court. They typically question their witnesses, cross-examine the other side's witnesses, and present other evidence.

In an appeal, the parties on each side of a case submit a **brief** to the court—a written document stating the party's arguments and legal basis for the case. Sometimes, appellate courts decide a case based only on the briefs, without lawyers appearing in court.

Sometimes, appellate courts allow the parties to make **oral arguments** in court. During oral arguments, lawyers from each side take turns standing before the judges and arguing the case. Judges often interrupt lawyers to fire questions at them. There is no witnesses testimony.

At some point after oral arguments, the judges deliberate on the case. Eventually, and it can take months, the appellate court will rule on the case and produce a written opinion.

## Circuit Courts' Effect on Law & Public Policy

A circuit court's ruling on a legal issue is the final word within the circuit, unless the Supreme Court invalidates the ruling. The Supreme Court hears very few cases, so most circuit court rulings stand. Thus, circuit courts often have an impact on public policy within their circuits.

### Where the Circuits Are

So far, Congress has created 13 federal appellate circuits: 12 encompass some states and territories, and 1 hears certain types of cases regardless of geography. Below is a list of the federal appellate circuits:

- **1st Circuit**: Maine, Massachusetts, New Hampshire, Puerto Rico.

- **2nd Circuit**: Connecticut, New York, Vermont.

- **3rd Circuit**: Delaware, New Jersey, Pennsylvania, U.S. Virgin Islands.

- **4th Circuit**: Maryland, the Carolinas, Virginia, West Virginia.

- **5th Circuit**: Louisiana, Mississippi, Texas.

- **6th Circuit**: Kentucky, Michigan, Ohio, Tennessee.

- **7th Circuit**: Illinois, Indiana, Wisconsin.

- **8th Circuit:** Arkansas, Iowa, Minnesota, Missouri, Nebraska, the Dakotas.

- **9th Circuit**: Alaska, Arizona, California, Guam, Hawaii, Idaho, Montana, Nevada, Northern Mariana Islands, Oregon, Washington.

- **10th Circuit:** Colorado, Kansas, New Mexico, Oklahoma, Utah, Wyoming.

- **11th Circuit**: Alabama, Florida, Georgia.

- **D.C. Circuit**: Washington, D.C.

- **Federal Circuit**: entire U.S., certain types of cases.

You can find out more about any circuit court by searching online for the specific court: for example, "federal court 9th circuit."

# The U.S. Supreme Court

## Supreme Court Justices

Judges on the Supreme Court are called "Justices." Currently, 9 Justices are on that Court: the Chief Justice and 8 Associate Justices. Congress decides the number of Justices by statute (U.S. Code, Title 28, Part I).

The Constitution gives presidents the power to appoint Justices, with Senate approval, but doesn't list qualifications for Justices. Yes, a President could appoint someone who has no legal training, but the Senate might not confirm that appointment. Checks and balances.

Presidents tend to appoint people to the U.S. Supreme Court who have served as judges or have a solid legal background. The current Justices' bios are at www.supremecourt.gov.

## What the Supreme Court Does

Mostly, the Supreme Court acts as an appellate court, like the circuit courts but at a higher level. The Supreme Court reviews cases from circuit courts and other federal courts. It can review state court cases involving federal law.

Below are examples of the types of cases the Supreme Court has jurisdiction over:

- Cases arising under the Constitution, other federal laws, or U.S. treaties
- Controversies in which the U.S. Government is a party
- Controversies between two or more U.S. states

The Constitution gives Congress the power to affect some aspects of the Supreme Court's jurisdiction (Article III, Section 2).

## Supreme Court's Effect on Public Policy

The Supreme Court affects law and public policy no matter what the Court does. When the Court chooses to not hear a case, the Court is allowing a lower court's decision to stand—which affects law and policy.

When the Supreme Court interprets the U.S. Constitution in a case, that ruling stands unless the Supreme Court reverses it later, like the Court did in the 1966 poll-tax case. Lower courts, Congress, and the President are bound by a Supreme Court ruling on the Constitution.

They are also bound by the Supreme Court's interpretation of statutes and regulations. However, if Congress doesn't like the Court's interpretation of a statute, Congress could repeal the statute or pass a new one.

## Caseload and the Court's Yearly Terms

For the most part, the Supreme Court chooses whether to hear cases. People petition the Court to hear a case, and the Justices vote on the petition.

These days, the Supreme Court receives over 7,000 petitions each year and chooses to hear less than 200 of them. Thus, it's not likely that a case will be heard by the Supreme Court.

The Supreme Court has yearly terms that start on the first Monday of each October and last until late June or early July. The Justices meet at the Supreme Court Building in D.C.

## Process for Supreme Court Review

People usually ask the Supreme Court to review another court's ruling by petitioning for what's called a **writ of certiorari**. If the Court "grants cert" (decides to hear the case), the parties on each side submit briefs.

Like the circuit courts of appeal, the Supreme Court decides some cases based only on the briefs. In other cases, the Supreme Court allows oral arguments, too.

The Justices vote on how to rule on cases. If at least 5 of the 9 Justices agree on how a case should be decided, there is a **majority opinion**. The majority's opinion is the Court's opinion. Often, one Justice will write the majority's opinion. Justices who disagree with the majority might write a **dissenting opinion** ("dissent" for short), explaining why they disagree with the majority.

The Court's opinions are published, so other courts, lawyers, and the public can read them. Supreme Court opinions are online at multiple places, including www.supremecourt.gov.

## Specialty Courts & Judges

Congress has created specialty courts that have limited jurisdiction to handle specific types of cases. Below are a few examples of those courts:

- Court of International Trade
- Foreign Intelligence Surveillance Court
- Tax Court
- Court of Appeals for the Armed Services
- Court of Appeals for Veterans Claims

Judges on those courts face different appointment processes and terms. For example, the President appoints judges to the Court of International Trade for life, with Senate approval. The Chief Justice of the Supreme Court appoints judges to the Foreign Intelligence Surveillance Court for 7-year terms.

## Administrative Law Judges

Administrative Law Judges (ALJs) are a different breed. They have judicial duties but **work for Executive Branch agencies**. ALJs often hold administrative hearings to decide disputes between an agency and people affected by that agency.

More than 30 federal agencies have ALJs. Examples include the Department of Labor, the Environmental Protection Agency, the Federal Communications Commission, and the Social Security Administration.

ALJs' decisions can be appealed, usually to an agency's appellate body. Eventually, an ALJ's decision could be reviewed by a Judicial Branch court, like a district or circuit court. Different agencies have different procedures for handling appeals.

## Judicial Branch Agencies

The Judicial Branch has a few agencies, including—

- The Administrative Offices of the U.S. Courts
- The U.S. Sentencing Commission
- The Supreme Court Police

The **Administrative Offices** support federal courts by providing legislative, technological, management, and budget-related services. The **Sentencing Commission** reports on criminal-sentencing practices and makes recommendations about those practices. The **Supreme Court Police** protect the Justices, the building, and people in the building.

# Part III

Influences on the
Government,
How It's Broken,
& How You Can
Help Fix It

# Chapter 6

## Outside Influences on Our Government & Corruption of the Process

### What this Chapter Covers:

#### Journalism & Media

- Why We Need a Free Press

- Media vs. Journalism

- Bias in the Press

- Profit Motive: Media & Advertisers

- Being Better Informed & Weeding out Garbage

#### Peaceful Protesting

#### Lobbying Government Officials

- Lobbying & Constitutional Rights

- Who Lobbies Government Officials

#### M-O-N-E-Y: Donations & Outside Spending

- Campaigns Cost a Lot

- Campaign Finance Laws and Problems

## Journalism & Media

### Why We Need a Free Press

The press (aka, the "Fourth Estate") was important to the Constitution's Framers, so they protected freedom of the press in the 1st Amendment. They knew that democracy and the Rule of Law depend on citizens holding government accountable, which requires citizens to be well informed and to vote knowledgeably.

We voters would be poorly informed if we relied only on messages crafted by government officials and their staff. That's why we need a Free Press.

Our history is full of examples of false propaganda, like messages about the Vietnam War and Watergate. The lead-up to the Iraq war is an example of what happens when the press is too frightened to report freely, as exposed in Bill Moyers' 2007 documentary, *Buying the War*. It's online.

Former President George W. Bush was crucified by the press. Yet, 8 years after he left office, he said in a TV interview that the Free Press is "indispensable to democracy" and followed up with this:

> We need the media to hold people like me to account.... It's important for the media to call to account people who abuse their power."

In other words, We the People need a watchdog to let us know what's really happening in our government and when the people running it are out of line.

### Media vs. Journalism

The terms "media" and "journalism" aren't the same. Journalists communicate through media—like TV, the Internet, or printed publications. But not all people publishing or broadcasting through the media are doing journalism.

People who sell gadgets on infomercials are media figures but aren't journalists. And that's okay because they aren't pretending to be journalists.

There are news reports, and there are editorials. **News reports** focus more on what happened, like Congress passing a law or a politician misbehaving and causing a scandal. **Editorials** focus more on someone's opinion about what happened.

There's nothing wrong with editorials. For some years, I regularly wrote guest editorials for my local newspaper. The 1st Amendment gives us ordinary folks and professional journalists a right to share our opinions.

One major problem: media outlets pretend to be doing news reports when they're actually doing editorials meant to manipulate your opinion. Many viewers don't know the difference and get duped into feeling well informed by people who knowingly leave out, twist, or lie about government-related information.

### Bias in the Press

Many news-media outlets seem to support certain types of public policy. Some favor policies and politicians that benefit working- and middle-class people. Some want to protect big businesses. Some favor open government, while others favor allowing officials to operate in secret. Those leanings are examples of **biases**.

Some degree of bias may have always existed among media outlets. Starting in 1949, government regulations reduced the bias of radio and TV broadcasters through the **Fairness Doctrine**, which required broadcasters to—

- Discuss controversial issues of public concern and
- Broadcast conflicting views about those issues.

The basic idea was that the government allowed broadcasters to profit from the "airwaves," which the public owns, so broadcasters should give the public the benefit of being well informed.

In 1987, **the Fairness Doctrine was abolished**. This enabled the growth of media outlets that heavily slant toward certain political agendas and do editorials disguised as news reports.

That's why it's so common now for some media outlets to leave out, twist, exaggerate, or lie about information to manipulate your opinions. The Internet has made matters worse.

Then there's **fake news**, meaning stories about things that didn't happen or just aren't true. If a story says that a senator murdered children, for example, search online for the politician's name + "murdered children." If you don't see rational reports at multiple media outlets about real law enforcement action—like an indictment or arrest—the story is likely fake.

### Profit Motive: Media Outlets & Advertisers

Most media outlets are for-profit businesses. Usually, the bigger their audience, the more an outlet can charge for ads. No judgement: that's just reality.

Some media outlets try to attract viewers by providing solid, useful information. Many viewers want that from their news.

Some outlets try to attract certain viewers by riling up emotions like fear, anger, and outrage. To rile up emotions, some outlets leave out truths, exaggerate truths, or just make things up. Seriously.

Advertisers can influence how some media outlets handle certain news stories or issues. Many big businesses spend millions each year on ads in various media, and media outlets want to keep the advertising dollars coming in. Upsetting advertisers is not a good way to do that. Keeping advertisers happy increases the chances that dollars will keep coming.

Let's say that certain chemical manufacturers and oil companies oppose certain anti-pollution laws that would cost a bit of money to comply with. One way to block such laws is for the industry groups to lobby government officials. Another way is to get people elected to office who oppose such laws. Donating money to industry-friendly candidates is one way to help do that.

Another way is to advertise with media outlets that are biased toward industry-friendly politicians and candidates. Yet another way is for advertisers to pressure media outlets to cover certain politicians and candidates in friendly or unfriendly ways.

Does that really happen? I'm not sure because I haven't been part of the conversations between media outlets and advertisers. But the motives exist, and it doesn't seem beyond possibility.

## Being Better Informed & Weeding Out Garbage

These days, it's hard to know whether a media story is accurate and complete. Even journalists who aren't trying to manipulate your opinion may leave out details due to time limits. Also, some journalists have better research skills than others.

The first step toward being better informed is to **read the entire article**, not just the first few paragraphs. Details toward the end of an article can be important.

**Don't rely on headlines**. They're short and don't contain much information. Also, some media outlets try to attract readers by using sensational headlines to rile up emotions. Some outlets use misleading headlines. Below are examples of what I mean:

- **Actual Events:** The U.S. President ordered a missile strike on a warehouse on 10 acres in Country X, where terrorists had stored weapons. The President warned Country X so it could evacuate civilians. The warehouse was destroyed but no civilians were injured.

- **Accurate Headline:** President Orders Missile Strike on Warehouse in Country X.

- **Sensational Headline**: President Starts World War III.

The accurate headline doesn't give details, like why the President chose to strike or that he warned the other country. You would have to read the article to find out. But the headline doesn't mislead readers or seek to rile up emotions.

The sensational headline incites people's fear. It's also inaccurate: the President didn't declare war (only Congress can do that). Yes, the warehouse bombing could trigger events that future historians might believe started what might turn out to be World War III. But when the headline was published, there were too many future unknowns for anyone to accurately say that the warehouse bombing started a massive war.

Another step toward being informed is to **be skeptical of media stories**. Don't assume that a story is true or complete just because you see it on TV or a snazzy website.

Some broadcasters and writers purposely leave out details or exaggerate facts to manipulate viewers' opinions. Rational criticism of politicians is fine, but watch out for irrational statements—especially those including **insults and emotion**. Here's an example of what I mean:

- **Irrational Statement**: Corrupt union-puppet Senator Smith voted for a bill that will starve your child.

- **Rational Statements**: Senator Smith upset constituents by voting for a bill that increases safety standards in frozen-food processing plants. The bill may increase the cost of frozen meals by 20 cents.

The irrational statement insults Senator Smith ("corrupt" and "puppet"). It stirs up readers' emotions by making them fear that their children will starve. It also lacks detail. Busy people who skim read might believe that Senator Smith is an evil ghoul who aims to harm kids for fun.

The rational example doesn't insult Senator Smith but does criticize the senator's vote (upset constituents and higher food costs). It also gives details, so readers can decide whether to be upset. Paying 20 cents more for a frozen meal might bother some people but not others.

To weed out biased stories, it helps to look at how multiple media outlets handle the same story. That's also a good way to gather more facts because different outlets might leave out different details about the same story.

If a certain media outlet repeatedly gets things wrong, don't rely on that outlet. If an outlet consistently gets things right, you can trust that outlet somewhat but still need to check multiple outlets for differing details.

As well as looking at multiple media outlets, you can look at fact-checking sites like **FactCheck** (www.factcheck.org). It's non-partisan, meaning it will point out anyone's flaws and errors. Sometimes you'll like what it says. Sometimes you won't. You can search FactCheck for issues or people.

**PolitiFact** (www.politifact.com) is another non-partisan website that has called out politicians and media from all sides. Yet another site is **Snopes** (www.snopes.com), which seems to focus more or debunking rumors and urban myths but does hit on politics.

**Wikipedia** (www.wikipedia.org) gives explanations about all sorts of things. People can anonymously add information to Wikipedia, and some contributors may be biased. The good thing is that many Wikipedia statements have footnotes that list the sources—the specific media outlets or books. If a source is an obviously biased media outlet, be skeptical.

Some fact-checking websites pose as unbiased and non-partisan but are the opposite. Below are a few things that should make you skeptical of sites labeled "fact checker":

- The site often insults or flatters certain politicians.
- Sources aren't listed.
- Internet sources are listed but not linked.

- Internet sources are linked but don't show the media outlet's name (you need to click to find out).

There are no guarantees that you'll weed out every morsel of bias or fakery. But checking media outlets and "fact checkers" will help you weed out some of the garbage.

Yes, it takes time. But it's **your only defense** against media outlets trying to dupe you into promoting their interests while working against your own.

## Peaceful Protesting

The 1st Amendment gives us the right "to petition the Government for a redress of grievances" and to assemble "peaceably." In other words, we have a constitutional right to protest what our government is doing.

"Peaceably" is the key word. It's illegal for people to gather and throw bricks at the Capitol Building. The Capitol Police can escort protestors out of the Senate visitor gallery for disrupting proceedings by yelling. But protestors could gather near the Capitol and protest by holding signs and chanting slogans.

In-person protests and marches are common in our history. During the Vietnam War, about 100,000 people gathered at the Lincoln Memorial to protest the war, and 30,000 marched from there to the Pentagon. Those protests played a part in our government's eventual withdrawal of troops from Vietnam.

In 2017, about 500,000 women and men went to D.C. for the "Women's March," the largest protest in U.S. history. Some people gave speeches, and some carried signs. They focused on issues like healthcare, workers' rights, racial equality, and women's issues. That day, over 2 million other people gathered in other cities for related protests.

That day, government officials saw The People waking up and making demands. That's what democracy is about.

In-person protests aren't the only kind. People can protest by signing petitions, in person or online. They can protest through group-organized emails, letters, or phone calls to government officials.

Protests are basically group-lobbying efforts. Protests put elected officials on notice that they'd better consider The People's voices if they want The People's votes.

## Lobbying Government Officials

### Lobbying & Constitutional Rights

**Lobbying** means trying to influence or persuade someone. The word "lobbyist" (someone who lobbies) started as slang for people who hung out in government-building lobbies, waiting to talk to officials who were passing through.

The 1st Amendment gives us a right to "petition the Government for a redress of grievances," meaning a right to try to influence our government. In other words, **we have a constitutional right to lobby**.

Lobbying is associated with corruption because for-profit lobbyists pour money into our political process and seem to get favors in return. That's why some people refer to for-profit lobbying as "legal bribery."

### Who Can Lobby Government Officials

### Individuals & Grassroots Groups

Any of us can lobby Members of Congress or officials at other levels of government. We can lobby officials or their staff directly through—

- Emails
- Letters
- Phone calls
- In-person visits

Scheduling meetings with Members of Congress isn't easy because they represent hundreds of thousands of people and have limited time. Presidents represent even more people.

It's easier to get access to officials' staffers, though they're busy, too. Staffers know things. Officials rely on staffers for information, so staffers have some influence on the officials they work for.

There is power in numbers, so many people lobby as part of a **grassroots group**: a group of ordinary citizens, as opposed to a political party or other organization. A grassroots group that starts with 5 people can grow to include thousands of members.

Grassroots groups can be very powerful. In the 60s and 70s, for example, grassroots efforts helped push our government to make changes, like ending the Vietnam War and promoting rights for people of all races.

Details about directly communicating with government officials are in Chapter 7. The tips apply whether you're communicating individually or as part of a group.

### Lobbyists for Hire

Some people lobby the government to promote the public's interest, like advocates for the environment or constitutional rights. That's called **public-interest lobbying**. There's not much money to be made from public-interest lobbying, yet some people make a career of it. They are professional lobbyists but are different from for-profit lobbyists.

**For-profit lobbyists** are "hired guns." They'll lobby for pretty much anyone who pays them. And they're not cheap: retainers can cost tens-of-thousands a month.

For-profit lobbying is big business. In 2016, over $3 billion was spent on lobbying the federal government. More than 11,000 people were registered to lobby the federal government, though some were public-interest lobbyists. That data is from the Center for Responsive Politics (www.crp.org).

Some lobbyists work individually or for lobbying firms. Some are in-house employees of an interest group or business that has a lobbying department—usually called "government relations," "government affairs," or "public affairs" departments.

Being an effective lobbyist requires **access** to government officials, basically meaning officials or key staffers will take phone calls from the lobbyist.

Access depends on building relationships with officials and staffers. Many lobbyists used to be government "insiders": elected officials, agency officials, or staffers. Becoming a lobbyist after leaving government is known as going through the **revolving door**.

The revolving door causes concern because some officials, while working in government, are tempted to create future job opportunities for themselves by ignoring The People's demands and doing favors for industries or businesses.

Here's an example. One Congressman—while on a House committee that dealt with drug companies—helped pass a law that was great for drug companies but bad for us taxpayers. After leaving Congress, he got a high-paying job with an industry group that represented (you guessed it) drug companies.

Coincidence? Maybe. But many people wondered if that Congressman had betrayed us taxpayers to push for his future personal gain.

**Lobbying bans** aim to delay or prevent government officials from going from government work to lobbying. The hope is that such bans will prevent government officials (while still in government) from favoring industries' interests over The People's interests. The effectiveness of lobbying bans is questionable.

Working in government is one way for people to build relationships that create access to government officials. Someone who moves from a government job to lobbying needs to maintain those relationships to maintain the access.

One way to maintain or increase access to elected officials is **raising money** for their campaigns. A lobbyist can't write a $100,000 check to a candidate's campaign because the law limits how much a person can donate directly.

Instead, a lobbyist might **bundle** smaller donations from multiple people—say, $2,000 donations from 50 people. In the candidate's eyes, the lobbyist gets credit for raising $100,000 for the campaign. Some Members of Congress might be inclined to take phone calls from lobbyists who can raise that kind of money.

Another way that lobbyists raise money is through **PACs** (political action committees). There's more about PACs later in this chapter.

As well as directly lobbying government officials, professional lobbyists might indirectly lobby officials through **ad campaigns** about certain issues. Ad campaigns can be effective because—

(1) They can reach the elected official.

(2) They can influence public opinion.

Public opinion matters to officials who want to get re-elected. An ad campaign might inspire constituents to pressure an official to take the action favored by the lobbyist who created the campaign.

Ad campaigns can cost millions. Many public-interest and grassroots groups can't afford the types of ad campaigns that some business or industry groups can.

Some people say that money buys access to elected officials, and there's some truth to that. Donations are covered later in this chapter.

Federal laws regulate lobbying activities, as do some House and Senate ethics rules. **Gift giving** is one example. It used to be common for lobbyists to give gifts to Members of Congress or their staffers, like expensive meals, Super Bowl tickets, or a week at a resort in the Bahamas. No kidding.

Back in the '90s, the House and Senate passed **gift-ban** rules. Basically, Members and employees of Congress can't accept expensive gifts from lobbyists.

But the gift ban doesn't solve the problem of money in politics. Instead of giving gifts, for-profit lobbyists pour money into Members' campaigns, PACs and other organizations (covered later in this chapter).

Lobbying is regulated at the federal and state levels, but different governments have different rules. Many governments require lobbyists to register before lobbying, to disclose whom they're lobbying in government, and to make periodic reports.

Various government entities have databases relating to lobbyists' reports, including the U.S. House and U.S. Senate. The Center for Responsive Politics also has lobbying databases (www.opensecrets.org/lobby) based on federal government data, like which businesses or groups lobbied which government offices and how much money certain industries or groups paid for lobbying.

### Interest Groups

Interest groups come in many flavors. If a lot of people care about an issue or cause, chances are there's an interest group lobbying for it. Some focus on specific issues or causes, like education, health care, or religion.

Many professions have interest groups that lobby government officials to benefit their professions. For example, the American Medical Association (AMA) advocates for doctors. The American Institute of CPAs (AICPA) advocates for accountants.

Some interest groups advocate for industries, largely to push for laws that translate into more money for an industry. For example, the Pharmaceutical Researchers and Manufacturers of America (PhRMA) advocates for drug companies. The U.S. Oil & Gas Association advocates for oil and natural-gas producers.

There are interest groups at the state and regional levels, too. Some interest groups can afford to employ in-house lobbyists. Some pay well-connected, for-profit lobbyists.

### Individual Businesses

Many big businesses spend money lobbying the government to shape the law in ways that help them make more money. Yes, it's that simple. A business is not likely to spend $5 million on lobbying efforts if it doesn't think it can make more than $5 million from the results.

Some businesses (like Microsoft and Exxon) are big enough to have their own in-house lobbyists. Some use outside lobbyists.

### Other Governments

State governors or legislators can lobby Congress, the President, or other U.S. government officials. Local governments can also lobby federal government officials—or state officials, for that matter.

Even foreign governments lobby U.S. government officials, through diplomats or paid lobbyists. There are laws relating to lobbyists who represent foreign governments to U.S. officials.

# M-O-N-E-Y: Donations & Outside Spending

### Campaigns for Federal Office Cost a Lot

Campaigns cost money because reaching voters through ads and campaign materials costs money. The more voters a candidate needs to reach, the more money it costs.

Most candidates for the U.S. House needs to reach hundreds of thousands of voters within their district. In the 2016 election, the average amount spent by U.S. House candidates' campaigns was about $1.3 million.

Most candidates for U.S. Senate need to reach millions of voters because they run in the whole state, not smaller districts. In 2016, the average amount spent by Senate candidates was over $10 million.

Presidents run for office in the entire nation, which has about 200 million voters. In 2016, Hillary Clinton's campaign committee spent about $560 million, and Donald Trump's spent about $325 million. Those amounts don't include money that outside groups spent supporting those candidates.

Money plays a huge part in our political process, so concerns about corruption are widespread and warranted.

**Campaign finance laws** are meant to reduce the potential for corruption by—

> (1)   limiting the amount of money donors can give and
>
> (2)   requiring candidates to report who donates directly to them.

Those laws have failed to reduce the amount of money that enters and corrupts our political system. Why? Because people have other, legal ways to pour money into it (more about that in the next section).

## Some Campaign Finance Laws Allow Corruption

Laws limit who can give directly to candidates and how much. For example, **corporations and labor unions can't donate directly to candidates** for federal office. But they have other ways to spend money to influence elections.

Below are a few examples of limits on how much money certain types of donors can give directly to a candidate for federal elections (2017-18):

- Individual Donor: $2,700
- Multi-candidate PAC: $5,000
- National Party Committee: $5,000

Those are per-election limits, meaning per primary, run-off, and general election. (National party committees can give more to Senate candidates.) The Federal Election Commission has more details about donation limits (www.fec.gov).

Donation limits aren't very limiting. For example, an individual could give $2,700 to a candidate and still give $5,000 to a **PAC** (political action committee). The PAC could then give some money to the candidate. There's an extra step, but more than $2,700 of that individual's money could go to the candidate.

There are other types of organizations that have no limits on how much money they can raise and spend, which makes donation limits for candidates almost meaningless. Examples of organizations include—

- Super PACs
- 527s
- 501(c)(4)s

The 527s and 501(c)(4)s are named for the numbered sections of our tax laws that regulate them.

**Super PACs** aren't really PACs. They're "independent expenditure-only committees," and they're regulated differently.

While PACs can give money to candidates, Super PACs can't. PACs can't take money from corporations or labor unions, but Super PACs can. There are limits on how much money PACs can take from donors, but **Super PACs can raise unlimited amounts** from corporations, people, and various groups.

A Super PAC can run ads that advocate for the election or defeat of candidates, as long as the Super PAC acts "independently" (doesn't coordinate its efforts with a candidate). But do they need to coordinate? Super PACs know how to run positive ads for candidates they support and negative ads for candidates they want to take down.

In 2016, almost 2,400 Super PACs were registered with the government. They raised about $1.8 billion and spent about $1.1 billion. Here are a few examples of Super PACs:

- Priorities USA Action (pro-Clinton)
- Rebuilding America Now (pro-Trump)
- Club for Growth Action (big business)
- National Association of Realtors
- League of Conservation Voters (environment)
- Senate Leadership Fund (Republicans)

Like other organizations, some PACs and Super PACs have straightforward names, like the National Association of Realtors. We know where that organization's interests lie.

Some groups have **misleading names**. For example, someone might name a Super PAC "Defenders of Freedom." But the name doesn't tell you what *type* of freedom it defends. The freedom to speak out? To hang out in nudist colonies? To dump chemical waste into a city's drinking water?

You can get clues about a Super PAC's or other group's agenda by looking at who the major donors are. If oil companies donated millions to "Defenders of Freedom," chances are the Super PAC supports oil-industry-friendly politicians or trashes politicians trying to limit what those companies do.

Super PACs and some other groups must disclose who donated money to them, so there's some transparency. People who have time to do research can **follow the money**—find out who funds a Super PAC and might be asking for favors from candidates who get elected.

Like Super PACs, **527s** can raise unlimited amounts of money and must publicly disclose their donors' names. One big difference is that Super PACs' ads can advocate for the election or defeat a candidate, while 527s' ads can't. Instead, 527s' ads focus on issues.

The **501(c)(4)s**, also called "social welfare groups," can spend money influencing elections *without* disclosing who gave them money. Some people call that **dark money** because the sources are hidden from us voters. Those groups are tax exempt, as long as their primary focus isn't politics.

Campaign finance law is complex. So are the loopholes that enable a few, well-funded people and groups to have such a huge influence on our elections.

At this point, we can't legally stop those few people or groups from trying to influence government. They too have 1st Amendment rights.

But we *can* reduce their influence on us by **refusing to blindly believe ads** paid for by PACs and other organizations, especially those with glorious names. The more outlandish, insulting, or dramatic an ad is—the more fear or anger it stirs up—the more skeptical you should be.

If you see such ads on TV or the Internet, you can mute the sound or refuse to click on them. In other words, you can boycott such ads.

Over the years, the federal government has made many attempts at reforming the campaign-finance system. Those attempts haven't fully succeeded, but our nation had made progress compared to where we were in the 1980s.

Then 2010 came along and with it the U.S. Supreme Court case, *Citizens United v. the Federal Election Commission*. By a 5-to-4 majority, the more corporate-friendly Justices struck down as unconstitutional some key pieces of our anti-corruption laws.

Among other things, the Court held that corporations have free-speech rights, like We the People do. This gave corporations a level of influence that they hadn't had for decades. The rise of Super PACs began after *Citizens United*.

One result: the relatively few Americans who can afford to spend millions influencing elections might have more say over our government than millions of other Americans do.

Another result is that ordinary Americans have been waking up to the reality of our system. They're taking an interest, getting involved, and pushing back. It'll take time, but we have a chance to fix some problems (more about that in Chapter 7).

# Chapter 7

# Ways You Can Help Influence & Fix the Government

---

### What this Chapter Covers:

## Voting Knowledgeably

- Why Voting Matters

- Getting Information about Candidates

- Make Sure You're Registered to Vote

- Find Out When & Where (it can change)

## Lobbying Elected Officials Politely

- Direct Contact

- Writing Letters to Newspapers

- Politeness and Brevity

## Volunteering for Candidates

## Getting Involved with a Political Party

## Donating to Candidates, Causes, & Parties

## Running for Office

## Your Voice Matters & Has Power

---

## Voting Knowledgeably

### Why Voting Matters

Voting is one way for you to have a say over who will affect your life and how. That's true about all levels of government: local, state, and federal.

The people who get elected will make decisions that **affect your life**, policies that impact things like—

- What kind of jobs are available
- How much money you make
- How much credit-card interest you pay
- Whether you can afford to retire
- How much your taxes are
- The cost of your healthcare
- Which opportunities you and your family have

Yes, voting takes time, but elections don't happen every month. If you (and other people with similar interests) vote knowledgeably, there's a better chance that the people who get elected will care about your interests.

### Getting Information about Candidates

#### Incumbents

It's easy to find information about **incumbents**—people already in office and running for re-election—because they have voting records and prior media coverage.

Incumbents' websites might give you a clue about where they stand on some issues, but websites are not a stopping point. Candidates' websites are meant to make candidates look good, and some are less truthful than others.

Online searches for news stories about candidates can help. **Checking multiple media sources** on the same story or issue will give you a better chance of learning where a candidate really stands.

**Attack ads** can contain seeds of the truth. They can also contain exaggerations and fake claims. The more outrageous an attack ad is, the more suspicious you should be. If you see an ad linking a candidate to a terrorist shooting, you should probably do some fact checking.

As mentioned in Chapter 6, FactCheck is a good starting point for checking out media stories (www.factcheck.org). Also, at least 5 websites are good for finding some types of objective information about people who've already held office:

- Project Vote Smart (votesmart.org)
- GovTrack (govtrack.us)
- Ballotpedia (ballotpedia.org)
- Center for Responsive Politics (opensecrets.org)
- Library of Congress (Congress.gov)

**Project Vote Smart** covers mostly federal and state officials. You can search for them by name and find their bios, voting histories, positions on issues, and funding sources.

**GovTrack** mostly covers Congress. You can look up members by name and find information like their votes on key bills, which committees they're on, and what kinds of bills they've sponsored.

**Ballotpedia** covers federal, state, and some local officials. It includes various indicators of their political stances.

The **Center for Responsive Politics** covers details about federal officials, including who donated money to them. The CRP is all about "following the money" and covers lobbying information.

**Congress.gov** covers legislative actions: bills, committee reports, and how each member voted on a certain bill.

## New Candidates

New candidates' websites are only a starting point—worthwhile for basics about the candidate's bio and where he or she stands on certain issues. Some candidates shoot straight about some issues: for example, a straight thumbs-up or thumbs-down on gun restrictions, government-funded healthcare, the county's one-cent sales tax for schools, etc.

Beware of broad promises, like "If elected, I'll get everyone a job" or "I'll lower your taxes." Even if the candidates are sincere, they might not understand the limits on their power once in office.

News stories and editorials can be good for getting some information about a new candidate's past and where she or he claims to stand on issues. Sometimes, you can get an idea of whether the candidate is in sync with you. It's a dice roll because new candidates don't have voting records in Congress (or the state legislature or city council, etc.).

As with incumbents, **question attack ads** against new candidates. Because candidates are public figures, people can say horrifying things about them and (usually) not get sued. Some ad sponsors are less interested in truth and more interested in stirring up your emotions, like some industry-backed Super PACs and 501(c)(4)s.

## Make Sure You're Registered to Vote

### Registering the First Time

Most states require people to be registered to vote before voting. **Some states make registering harder than it needs to be**, even though voting is a constitutional right.

For example, Florida requires people to register at least 29 days before an election to vote in it, and registration is only in person or by mail. Georgia has a similar deadline but also allows online registration. Alabama is easier: the deadline is 15 days in advance, and registration can be in person, by mail, or online.

Some states offer automatic registration through certain government agencies, like the driver's license office. Details vary from state to state. You can check by contacting your county election office or searching online.

If your state requires you to submit forms to register to vote—

- Check the deadline through your county election office.
- Submit the forms a couple of months before the next election.
- Follow up because your registration may not be valid until the election office approves it.

A **felony conviction** can be another barrier to registering to vote. In most states, a person convicted of a felony loses the right to vote until that right is restored. Most states automatically restore people's rights after the sentence is served.

Some states require people to get the governor or a court to restore their rights. As of this writing, 9 states require people to jump through hoops to get their voting rights back after they paid their debt to society:

- Alabama
- Arizona
- Florida
- Iowa
- Kentucky
- Mississippi
- Nevada
- Virginia
- Wyoming

Maine and Vermont don't take away voting rights based on criminal convictions.

To find out how your state handles those things, call or email your county election office.

## Voter Purges: The Need to Check Your Registration

Registering once is all it should take. Again, voting is a constitutional right.

But some people's names get taken off the voter rolls because some states systematically **purge** the rolls. Those states claim that they purge voter rolls to reduce voter fraud by removing the names of people who've died or moved or are otherwise ineligible to vote. In reality, most states don't have huge numbers of dead or ineligible people voting.

Mistakes have occurred in some voter purges, causing thousands of truly eligible voters' names to be mistakenly removed. Some states have removed people from voter rolls simply because those people didn't vote in a few elections. No kidding.

Florida, Georgia, Michigan, Ohio, Pennsylvania, and Tennessee are examples of states that have faced voter-purging errors. In Florida, more than 1,000 people were wrongly purged from voter rolls before Election 2000 because they were mistakenly thought to be felons.

Why did that happen? Because some non-felons had similar names as actual felons, like Christine Smith versus Christopher Smith. Unfortunately, the computers—or the people operating them—didn't check it out well enough to prevent the errors.

Some states' voter purges have been riddled with problems, which resulted in lawsuits. To see whether your state has faced such problems, search online for "voter purge" + your state.

Some people who were wrongly purged from voter rolls didn't know it until they showed up to vote in an election. Most people don't get wrongly removed from voter rolls. Just to be safe, it couldn't hurt to check on your registration before the next election.

## Update Your Information if You Move

Even if you move to a new place within the same county, you can prevent hassles by letting the election office know. If nothing else, changing your address may change the place where you vote.

If you move to a new county or state, you'll probably need to register to vote there. To find your county election office, search online for "election office" + your county + your state.

## Find Out When & Where to Vote (It Can Change)

Many states have early voting and one official Election Day. Lines tend to be longer on Election Day. To find out if there's early voting and when Election Day is, contact your county election office or check its website.

Many counties are divided into **precincts** (areas within the county). Usually, voters from each precinct vote in a certain **polling place**, like a government building or church.

Polling places can change. In the last election, you might have voted at the Elks Lodge. In the next election, you might vote at the church down the road. To make sure that you don't waste time going to the wrong polling place, check with your election office before each election.

**Precinct consolidation** (assigning one polling place for multiple precincts' voters) is common these days. The stated reason for consolidating precincts is to save money, as it costs more to operate 52 polling places than 49.

Because more people show up to a polling place that serves multiple precincts, the downside of precinct consolidation is that some voters must —

- Travel farther to vote
- Face parking problems
- Wait longer in voting lines

While cost is a genuine concern, one result of precinct consolidation is that many lower-income voters are less likely to vote because they can't make the time to travel farther or wait in line longer. Early voting can be a solution to that problem in states that offer it.

Some states have passed or pushed for laws allowing precinct consolidation, including Florida, Georgia, North Carolina, and Ohio. Polling-place changes are likely in states that do precinct consolidation. To see if such laws have passed in your state, search online for "precinct consolidation" + your state.

## Lobbying Elected Officials Politely

### Direct Contact

### Finding the Right Officials

Whether you want to lobby Congress, your state legislature, or your city commission, find out (1) which official is the right one and (2) how to contact him or her. In most cases, you can find that information online or by phone.

To find your members of **Congress**, go to www.house.gov and www.senate.gov. To find your **state legislators**, try your county election office's website. If that doesn't give you the answer, search online for "legislature" + your state and look for a link about finding your representative.

To find elected officials at the **city or county level**, try your county election office. Some cities' and counties' elected officials represent only people in certain districts in the city or county. Other officials represent all people in the county or city. The same is true of School Board members in some states.

If your election office website doesn't have the information you seek, search online for "elected officials" + your county + your state.

### Email or Phone

Communicating with elected officials costs nothing but a little time. Doing so might help you get what you want.

Your elected officials represent all their constituents, even the ones who didn't vote for them. Officials who want to get re-elected care about what their constituents want, including you.

But elected officials can't know what you want if you don't tell them. If your members of Congress are about to vote on a bill you have an opinion about, you could tell them how you'd like them to vote and why. If your child had a problem at a public school and the principal didn't solve it, you might contact your School Board member.

Most elected officials want to know their constituents' opinions because officials can get voted out of office if they misunderstand constituents. That's why many officials have their staff read emails, take calls, and organize the information.

Some years back, a state legislator told me that when she got a constituent's email stating a certain opinion, she assumed that 5,000 other people had the same opinion but didn't email her. Other elected officials might similarly view constituents' messages. If your elected officials do, then your email or phone call may carry more weight than you'd thought.

Communications to public officials may be part of the public record. For that reason, **don't put personal details in an email that you don't want other people to find out**.

### Private Meetings

The larger an elected official's constituency is, the harder it is to schedule a private meeting. It's easier in smaller counties and cities. If you get an offer to meet with a staffer, take it. Staffers tend to know a lot and can get things done.

If you get a private meeting, don't be nervous. Most elected officials and their staff are pleasant—it's part of being public servants. If you're polite with them, most of them will be polite with you (more about politeness later).

Whether you meet with an elected official or staffer, make a list beforehand of what you want to say or ask. Those people have limited time, so make the most of it.

## Watching Legislative Bodies' Meetings

You can watch Congress or your state legislature in session, but people usually can't speak out unless invited to do so beforehand. At public meetings of many city and county commissions, citizens can speak.

In my city, for example, I disliked a proposal to turn one 4-lane road into a 2-lane road. It wasn't a sexy issue, but I didn't want traffic to become even more irritating than it already was.

On the night that my City Commission was going to vote on the proposal, I went to that Commission meeting. So did about 100 other people. We each got a couple of minutes to stand up at a microphone and tell the commissioners what we thought. So many citizens showed up to speak that the citizen-comment part of the meeting took 4 hours.

The Commission was surprised by how many people came out against shrinking the road. The result: instead of quickly voting to pass the proposal, the Commission delayed the vote.

The point: citizens' opinions directly influenced my City Commission. And citizens' opinions can affect elected officials at all levels. Speaking up doesn't guarantee that you'll get what you want, but it does increase the chances.

Different local governments have different rules about when and how citizens can participate at meetings. You can get that information at your local government's website, by email, or by phone.

## Writing Letters to Newspapers

Many elected officials read newspapers' editorial (opinion) sections—or have staff read them—to get an idea of their constituents' opinions. I knew one state legislator whose staff regularly gathered newspapers' editorial pages from around the state so he could see what constituents in different areas wanted.

If you feel strongly about an issue, consider writing to your newspaper. Letters to a newspaper can have a double impact, compared to emails:

(1)  Elected officials learn what you want.

(2)  They know your letter might persuade thousands of readers who vote.

Here are a few tips, in case you want to try writing a letter to a newspaper:

- Avoid personal insults.
- Avoid emotional ranting.
- Instead, rationally state your opinion.
- Follow the newspaper's rules for submitting letters.
- It's okay to say that you disagree with an official, but do it civilly.

Some newspapers print emotional rants, but people who write in a calm and civil tone are taken more seriously.

**Don't put personal details** in a letter that you don't want thousands of people to know about. The letters are usually published in the newspaper's print version and online, so your letter could come up in Internet searches.

Many newspapers make it easy to submit letters. You can find submission guidelines at your newspaper's editorial page or website. You can also see sample letters by reading a newspaper's editorial section.

### Politeness and Brevity

When communicating to an elected official or staffer, be polite and be as brief as you can while stating the necessary info. If you want to rant or vent emotions, do it with a friend.

If you communicate with officials or staffers, you probably want something, like for them to vote a certain way or help you with something. Long emails or speeches with unnecessary details make it harder for people to grasp your message. **Get to the point**.

Rude, snarky, or ranty comments might amuse friends, but they can make strangers feel defensive. People who feel defensive are less likely to put serious effort into helping you.

## Volunteering for Candidates

Whether federal, state or local, most candidates like volunteers. I've volunteered for a few campaigns and found it enjoyable and rewarding. I also got 3 major benefits:

- Increasing the chance that people I agreed with would get elected
- Learning about issues and the political process
- Meeting nice people with common interests

Whether you like working with other people or alone, many campaigns will have something for you to do. Campaigns have different types of tasks for volunteers, like—

- Stuffing envelopes
- Holding a sign on a street corner
- Driving people to polls on election day
- Working on a campaign website or ads

- Contacting people to ask for donations or votes
- Delivering yard signs
- Hosting a meet-and-greet

As a volunteer, you can choose which tasks you're comfortable with, or you could say "I'm up for anything." Most candidates say yes to free help.

**Research a candidate before volunteering**. My first time, I volunteered for a local candidate's campaign because a friend supported him and the candidate was a nice guy. After listening to the candidate at a few meetings, I realized that his stance on important issues was very different from mine.

A few weeks later, I quit and volunteered for a candidate that was more in sync with me. If I'd researched the first candidate's positions beforehand, I could've saved time and avoided awkwardness.

Before volunteering, **go to a meet-and-greet** (fundraiser), which is a short social event. You don't have to donate or commit to volunteering. Just show up and enjoy meeting some people. Candidates and their supporters tend to be welcoming. Candidates' websites usually list the meet-and-greets.

If you want to volunteer for a candidate, contact campaign staff. The contact information should be on the candidate's website.

## Getting Involved with a Political Party

If interested, you could get involved with a political party. As with choosing a candidate, do some research beforehand. Go to some local-party meetings to help you decide whether to join or volunteer.

A good starting point is the local level of the party that interests you. Check to see whether the party has a county or city organization.

To find out how a party is organized in your state, check the **state-party website**: for example, the Connecticut Democratic Party, the Republican Party of New Mexico, or the Green Party of Oklahoma. The state-party website should have contact information for local party organizations.

If you're not sure which party is a good fit for you, do some research. There are many political parties, some not so well known. You could find parties through an online search.

Parties' websites are only a starting point because they are basically ads, meant to make a party look good to everyone. Thus, they don't always accurately state the party's real goals. No party's website will admit, "We don't care about people who work for low wages," even if the party habitually works against those workers' interests.

A party's website might state stances on specific issues, like school prayer or universal healthcare. Parties are less likely to state concrete details about their stance on broad issues like the economy. Instead, some parties address broad issues in vague, positive-sounding terms. A lot of it is useless to people trying to learn about a party.

To get a feel for what a party stands for **look at its actions, not its words**. For example, research how each party in Congress voted on controversial bills about certain issues, like healthcare, Internet neutrality, or whatever issues matter to you. Look at which party controlled Congress during certain periods when you liked or disliked how things were going (Chapter 3 has a table showing just that).

Research what types of people presidents from each party have appointed to agencies and courts. Check out websites like Project Vote Smart (votesmart.org) and Ballotpedia (ballotpedia.org).

If you read other people's opinions about a political party, be skeptical if you come across nasty insults or intense emotions, like fear or anger—as opposed to rational statements of disagreement.

Read multiple rational sources. There is no guarantee that your research will give you all the answers, but it will help you figure out which party is more in sync with your interests and beliefs.

Of course, you don't have to be involved with any political party to try to influence and help fix our government.

## Donating to Candidates, Causes & Parties

Some people don't have time for volunteer work. Another way to influence what happens in our nation is to donate money—even small amounts—to candidates, political parties, or causes. To find out which people or groups are in sync with you, do some research.

## Running for Office

### Yes, You Can (Probably)

There aren't many restrictions on who can and can't run for office. It's not like applying for a heart surgeon's job: candidates don't need a certain college degree or license. Candidates aren't required to have prior experience in office.

There are some basic requirements, but most people can meet them—if not now, in the future. For example, to be on a city council, you'd probably have to be a registered voter and might have to live in a certain district in the city. To be a U.S. Senator, you'd have to be at least 30 years old.

The requirements vary based on the position and level of government. If a certain elected office interests you, find out the basic requirements before you put a lot of effort into running.

## Why Some People Run for Office

### People Who Don't Seriously Try to Win

A man in a black cape has a tall black cylinder covering his head. He looks like a cartoon character. He's on stage with dignified candidates, debating before national media. His name is **Lord Buckethead**, a self-styled "intergalactic lord" from outer space. In 2017, he ran against the British Prime Minister.

Lord Buckethead got only 249 votes out of 32 million, but he also got major media spotlight. And he used that spotlight to seriously criticize government policies (and say absurd things). Here's one of his gems: "Stop selling arms to Saudi Arabia. Start buying lasers from Lord Buckethead."

In the U.S., many candidates have run for office who weren't seriously trying to win, though most didn't wear a costume. Such candidates had other reasons for running, like raising the public's awareness of certain issues or influencing how voters feel about certain policies or politicians.

Some candidates run as **spoilers**, to take votes from another candidate. For example, a spoiler wanting to take votes from a Republican city-council candidate would campaign to appeal to Republican voters but would run under a different party or no party. Spoilers have affected elections for both major U.S. parties.

You could choose to run for office as a spoiler or issue candidate, even an outrageous one like Lord Buckethead. Just make sure that what you want to accomplish is worth the effort you need to put into running.

Also, consider that running as a spoiler or issue candidate could help—or hurt—your chances of winning elections in the future if you ever run seriously. That depends partly on how you behave when campaigning.

## People Who Do Seriously Try to Win

Candidates who seriously try to win elections have different reasons for running. Some run because they support or oppose certain policies. I ran for School Board once because I believed I could help improve education by getting on the board and voting to put more money into classrooms.

Some people run for office because they like the idea of public service. Others want media exposure or political experience to make it easier to run for higher offices later.

Still other people run for office for eventual financial gain, but those candidates don't usually admit it publicly. A candidate for state legislature might run simply to push for laws that help her industry, like the insurance industry. Some people run to get career opportunities down the road in government, business, or lobbying.

Before you run for office, figure out your reasons. Decide whether the benefits are worth your efforts because positioning yourself to win an election takes a lot of time and work.

### Possible Benefits of Running

Whether candidates win or lose, they get the benefit of being part of something with real-world consequences. That, alone, is an accomplishment.

Unless they act like jerks while campaigning, even candidates who lose accomplish at least three things—

- Building a network of supporters
- Gaining campaign experience
- Getting media exposure (name recognition)

All three of those accomplishments can put candidates in a good position to run again, even if they lost the last election.

I didn't win my election, but I reaped benefits from running. I got to know good people. The experience and network I gained put me in a good position to run for office again, though I chose a different path.

The point: merely running for office can bring benefits. You can anticipate some of them (like network building), but other benefits might surprise you.

## Basic Process for Getting Elected

The processes for candidates vary depending on the level of government and the specific office. Here's a basic outline of the typical process:

- Qualifying for office
- Opening a campaign bank account
- Raising money
- Campaigning (while raising more funds)
- Filing campaign reports
- Opening Champagne on Election Day (or not)

**Qualifying** to run for office usually involves filing paperwork, getting voters' signatures, and maybe paying a fee—all by a certain deadline. Federal, state, and local governments have different processes.

Opening a **campaign account** is simple. Different banks and levels of government may have different policies.

**Raising money** is crucial, unless you can fund your own campaign. There are laws at every level of government about raising and spending campaign funds. Candidates need to learn about those laws. **It's not as hard as it might seem**: thousands of candidates had no clue about campaign-finance laws before they started running, but they learned.

**Campaigning** can involve many activities, like—

- Producing and delivering printed signs
- Designing, printing, and mailing flyers

- Designing and placing ads (TV, radio, Web)
- Doing candidate forums (like debates)
- Attending meet-and-greets

Many candidates must periodically **file reports** stating how much money their campaign raised and spent. The federal, state and local governments have different requirements.

## Choosing Which Office to Run for

There's no rule saying you must run for local office before running for state or federal office. If you already have big support networks and funding sources, you might win an election for higher office your first time out.

First-time candidates **usually start at the local level** because it's a good way to learn and tends to cost less than running at the state or federal level. It's easier to campaign for 10,000 voters in a small town than for 500,000 voters in a congressional district.

Basically, the more voters your campaign needs to target, the bigger the network of supporters you'll need. Big support networks can help you reach out to potential voters and help raise money to pay for ads, signs, T-shirts, etc. If your campaign is targeting a million voters, you would need help—volunteers or paid staff.

Because most candidates start by running for local offices, the rest of this chapter focuses on local government. To find out which elected offices exist in your area, search online for a list of elected officials in your county and city. You'll probably find offices like these:

- City Council
- County Council
- School Board
- Tax Collector
- Property Appraiser

- State (or District) Attorney
- Public Defender
- Sheriff

To see what certain elected officials deal with, check out their websites. For elected officials that vote and attend meetings—like school board or city council—look at some meeting **agendas** (lists of issues they plan to address) or some **minutes** (things they did at past meetings).

To get a better feel for what local elected officials do, **watch some meetings** of the council, commission, or board that interests you. You could go in person or watch via TV or Internet if they are broadcast in your area. Check the council's or board's website for meeting dates and agendas.

**Local newspapers** are another source of information that can help you understand what city and county governments do. News stories tend to focus on what elected officials did, like "Commissioner Smith voted for the sales-tax increase." Editorials and letters to the editor express people's opinions about what elected officials did, like "Commissioner Smith should be voted out of office for supporting the sales-tax increase." It's all worth looking at if you want to run for office.

If your state legislature interests you, start at its website. Look for recent bills to see what your representatives have been doing. Check out reputable newspapers in your state: many have sections on state government.

### Learning about Issues

As a candidate, you would need to know which issues concern the voters you're targeting and where you stand on those issues. Here's a list of resources that can help you learn about issues relevant to running for local office:

- Newspapers (news and editorial sections)
- Websites

- Political parties
- Activist groups
- Meetings of the elected body

Being knowledgeable doesn't guarantee that you will win an election. But understanding issues increases the chances that voters will see you as a worthwhile candidate.

## Building Support Networks

Support networks are important because people recognizing your name and thinking positively of you will make it easier for you to get votes. Support networks can help candidates—

- Attract volunteers
- Raise money
- Persuade other people to vote for them

Some people already have **non-political support networks** through involvement with business or professional groups, charity work, churches, clubs, sports leagues, etc. Most voters don't hang out in political circles, and you want their votes. Involvement in your community can help with that.

The most direct way to **build political support networks** is to be politically active:

- Volunteer for candidates' campaigns.
- Get involved with a political party.
- Get involved with causes, like the environment or health-care—whatever interests you.

If you want to run for office but don't have enough support networks, it'll take time to build them. Becoming politically active would be a good start, but don't avoid non-political activities.

Before committing to political activities, check things out. Go to some candidates' meet-and-greets. Sit in on some meetings of a local political party. Go to some issue groups' events.

By checking things out, you'll probably learn about issues. You may get a better idea of what sorts of candidates and issues are in sync with you. If nothing else, you'll probably meet some nice people and have a decent time.

## Raising Money

Money is necessary for political campaigns. That's the reality even for non-corrupt candidates.

Candidates rely on ads and other campaign materials to get their name out and project a good image to voters. Candidates can't have long chats with thousands of people during a campaign. Except in tiny towns, candidates can't even shake hands with most voters. There isn't enough time.

Yard signs, car signs and mailers are typical ways to reach out to voters—as are ads through the Internet, TV, radio, or mail. Those things cost M-O-N-E-Y.

Candidates who can't bring themselves to ask for money don't usually raise as much as candidates who can—unless they hire staff or find volunteers to ask for money. Most candidates who need to raise money need to be okay with asking for it. You can find courses on fundraising online or through your political party.

Campaign-finance laws restrict how candidates raise money (from whom and how much) and how they spend the money. Some laws require candidates to report the money that comes in and goes out.

The federal government has campaign-finance laws, as do many state and local governments. Your local elections office is a good place to start learning about the laws that apply to running for office.

## Running Against Incumbents

Incumbents have advantages that many first-time candidates don't, like name recognition and media exposure. On the flipside, incumbents have a record of actions that might have angered voters.

It's easier to run against a disliked incumbent than a well-liked one. I ran against a well-liked incumbent and lost. I knew there was a good chance I'd lose but ran anyway, knowing that even if I lost I would raise public awareness about how my School Board was spending money.

Whether you choose to run against an incumbent or wait for an open seat depends on (1) the political climate in your area, (2) the strength of your support networks, and (3) your funding options. Again, even if you lose an election, running a good and clean campaign can put you in a good position to run for office later.

## Downsides: Privacy Loss & Some Negativity

Candidates for public office give up some privacy because they must disclose some personal info. I had to disclose my debts and assets, and the local paper published that data.

Negativity comes if opponents dig for information they can use against a candidate. It's called **opposition research**, and many campaigns do it. Maybe they find a picture on social media from 10 years ago of a candidate burning a flag at a protest. Maybe they search public records and find that a candidate was arrested for a DUI on high-school graduation night.

Such things wouldn't necessarily stop you from winning an election, depending on how you handle the issues in the media. If you don't want such cans of worms opened publicly, then **running for office might not be for you**.

When I ran for office, my opponent and I ran clean campaigns—no ugliness or personal attacks. I did criticize some of her actions as a School Board member, but I did it rationally and civilly. We never attacked each other.

Not all candidates run clean campaigns. Some will do anything to win. If they can't find real "negatives" about an opponent, they'll exaggerate truths beyond recognition or even make stuff up. And you never know whether a candidate will do those things until after attack ads are launched.

The point is this: **you need to have a thick skin** to run for office. You need to be okay with negative publicity and be prepared to respond if appropriate.

If you're okay with some privacy loss and possible negative publicity, you might consider running for office. If not, you could stick to other ways of influencing what happens in your government(s) and trying to fix things.

## Your Voice Matters & Has Power

Our government affects you personally, whether you realize it or not. And you can affect government. You even have a constitutional right to try.

For years, only a small minority of Americans paid attention to what the government did. Some people lacked time or interest. Some believed their votes or lobbying efforts wouldn't make a difference—they believed their voice didn't matter.

One result: our government has spent decades protecting a small minority of vocal (usually well-funded) people at the expense of most Americans.

Over the past 30 years, more and more middle-class Americans—despite years of hard work—find themselves lacking financial security, good healthcare, and life-improving opportunities for their families.

In recent years, many Americans have awakened. They're paying attention to what our government does. They're exercising their right to participate, in big ways and small. They're finding their voice and getting results.

Decisions that affect your life are made by the people who participate in the process. There are many ways for you to participate, and any of them can bring about change.

Your vote matters. So does your voice, and it's powerful.

# Appendix

# Text of The United States Constitution

The document text below is from the National Archives' transcript of the U.S. Constitution. It's the original text, as you can tell from the old-style spelling, phrasing, and punctuation.

The Constitution doesn't have descriptive headings. I added headings and bolded some text to make it easier for you to find things. I also added a few explanations and other words. Any added words are in **brackets** that look like this: [ ].

## THE DOCUMENT'S TEXT

### [Preamble]

**We the People** of the United States, in Order to form a more perfect Union, establish Justice, insure domestic Tranquility, provide for the common defence, promote the general Welfare, and secure the Blessings of Liberty to ourselves and our Posterity, **do ordain and establish this Constitution** for the United States of America.

## Article I

### [Congress]

**Section. 1.**

All **legislative Powers** herein granted shall be vested in a **Congress** of the United States, which shall consist of a Senate and House of Representatives.

**Section. 2.**

The **House of Representatives** shall be composed of Members **chosen every second Year** by the People of the several States, and the Electors in each State shall have the Qualifications requisite for Electors of the most numerous Branch of the State Legislature.

No Person shall be a Representative who shall not have attained to the **Age of twenty five** Years, and been s**even Years a Citizen** of the United States, and who shall not, when elected, be an **Inhabitant of that State** in which he shall be chosen.

Representatives and direct Taxes shall be apportioned among the several States which may be included within this Union, according to their respective Numbers, which shall be determined by adding to the whole Number of free Persons, including those bound to Service for a Term of Years, and excluding Indians not taxed, three fifths of all other Persons.

> [The underlined text in the preceding paragraph was replaced or affected by 14th and 16th Amendments].

The actual Enumeration shall be made within three Years after the first Meeting of the Congress of the United States, and within every subsequent Term of ten Years, in such Manner as they shall by Law direct. The Number of Representatives shall not exceed one for every thirty Thousand, but each State shall have at Least one Representative; **and until such enumeration shall be made,** the State of New Hampshire shall be entitled to chuse three, Massachusetts eight, Rhode-Island and Providence Plantations one, Connecticut five, New-York six, New Jersey four, Pennsylvania eight, Delaware one, Maryland six, Virginia ten, North Carolina five, South Carolina five, and Georgia three.

> [About the underlined text above: the number of representatives has changed since the 1700s.]

When **vacancies** happen in the Representation from any State, the Executive Authority thereof shall issue Writs of Election to fill such Vacancies.

The House of Representatives shall chuse their **Speaker** and other Officers; and shall have the sole **Power of Impeachment.**

### Section. 3.

**The Senate** of the United States shall be composed of two Senators from each State, chosen by the Legislature thereof, for **six Years;** and each Senator shall have one Vote.

> [The underlined text in the preceding paragraph was replaced or affected by the 17th Amendment: senators are now elected by The People.]

Immediately after they shall be assembled in Consequence of the first Election, they shall be divided as equally as may be into three Classes. The Seats of the **Senators of the first Class** shall be vacated at the Expiration of the second Year, of the **second Class** at the Expiration of the fourth Year, and of the **third Class** at the Expiration of the sixth Year, so that one third may be chosen every second Year; and if Vacancies happen by Resignation, or otherwise, during the Recess of the Legislature of any State, the Executive thereof may make temporary Appointments until the next Meeting of the Legislature, which shall then fill such Vacancies.

> [The underlined text in the preceding paragraph was replaced or affected by the 17th Amendment.]

No Person shall be a Senator who shall not have attained to the **Age of thirty Years**, and been **nine Years a Citizen** of the United States, and who shall not, when elected, be an **Inhabitant of that State** for which he shall be chosen.

The **Vice President** of the United States shall be **President of the Senate**, but shall have no Vote, unless they be equally divided.

The Senate shall chuse their other Officers, and also a **President pro tempore**, in the Absence of the Vice President, or when he shall exercise the Office of President of the United States.

The **Senate shall have the sole Power to try all Impeachments**. When sitting for that Purpose, they shall be on Oath or Affirmation. When the President of the United States is tried, the Chief Justice shall preside: And no Person shall be convicted without the Concurrence of two thirds of the Members present.

Judgment in Cases of **Impeachment** shall not extend further than to removal from Office, and disqualification to hold and enjoy any Office of honor, Trust or Profit under the United States: but the Party convicted shall nevertheless be liable and subject to Indictment, Trial, Judgment and Punishment, according to Law.

**Section. 4.**

The **Times, Places and Manner of holding Elections** for Senators and Representatives, shall be prescribed in each State by the Legislature thereof; but the Congress may at any time by Law make or alter such Regulations, except as to the Places of chusing Senators.

The **Congress shall assemble** at least once in every Year, and such Meeting shall be on the first Monday in December, unless they shall by Law appoint a different Day.

> [The underlined text in the preceding paragraph was replaced or affected by 20th Amendment.]

**Section. 5.**

Each House shall be the Judge of the **Elections, Returns and Qualifications** of its own Members, and a Majority of each shall constitute a Quorum to do Business; but a smaller Number may adjourn from day to day, and may be authorized to compel the Attendance of absent Members, in such Manner, and under such Penalties as each House may provide.

Each House may determine the **Rules of its Proceeding**s, punish its Members for disorderly Behaviour, and, with the Concurrence of two thirds, expel a Member.

Each House shall keep a **Journal of its Proceedings**, and from time to time publish the same, excepting such Parts as may in their Judgment require Secrecy; and the Yeas and Nays of the Members of either House on any question shall, at the Desire of one fifth of those Present, be entered on the Journal.

Neither House, during the Session of Congress, shall, without the Consent of the other, **adjourn** for more than three days, nor to any other Place than that in which the two Houses shall be sitting.

## Section. 6.

The Senators and Representatives shall receive a **Compensation** for their Services, to be ascertained by Law, and paid out of the Treasury of the United States. They shall in all Cases, except Treason, Felony and Breach of the Peace, be **privileged from Arrest** during their Attendance at the Session of their respective Houses, and in going to and returning from the same; and for any Speech or Debate in either House, they shall not be questioned in any other Place.

No Senator or Representative shall, during the Time for which he was elected, be appointed to any civil Office under the Authority of the United States, which shall have been created, or the Emoluments whereof shall have been encreased during such time; and no Person holding any Office under the United States, shall be a Member of either House during his Continuance in Office.

## Section 7.

All **Bills for raising Revenue** shall originate in the House of Representatives; but the Senate may propose or concur with Amendments as on other Bills.

Every **Bill** which shall have passed the House of Representatives and the Senate, shall, before it become a Law, be **presented to the President** of the United States; If he approve he shall sign it, but if not he shall return it, with his Objections to that House in which it shall have originated, who shall enter the Objections at large on their Journal, and proceed to reconsider it. If after such Reconsideration two thirds of that House shall agree to pass the Bill, it shall be sent, together with the Objections, to the other House, by which it shall likewise be reconsidered, and if approved by two thirds of that House, it shall become a Law. But in all such Cases the Votes of both Houses shall be determined by yeas and Nays, and the Names of the Persons voting for and against the Bill shall be entered on the **Journal** of each House respectively. If any Bill shall not be returned by the President within ten Days (Sundays excepted) after it shall have been presented to him, the Same shall be a Law, in like Manner as if he had signed it, unless the Congress by their Adjournment prevent its Return, in which Case it shall not be a Law.

Every Order, Resolution, or Vote to which the Concurrence of the Senate and House of Representatives may be necessary (except on a question of Adjournment) shall be presented to the President of the United States; and before the Same shall take Effect, shall be approved by him, or being disapproved by him, shall be repassed by two thirds of the Senate and House of Representatives, according to the Rules and Limitations prescribed in the Case of a Bill.

### Section 8. [Enumerated powers of Congress]

The **Congress shall have Power** To lay and collect **Taxes, Duties, Imposts and Excises**, to **pay the Debts** and provide for the **common Defence** and **general Welfare** of the United States; but all Duties, Imposts and Excises shall be uniform throughout the United States;

To **borrow Money** on the credit of the United States;

To **regulate Commerce** with foreign Nations, and among the several States, and with the Indian Tribes;

To establish an uniform Rule of **Naturalization**, and uniform Laws on the subject of **Bankruptcies** throughout the United States;

To **coin Money**, regulate the Value thereof, and of foreign Coin, and fix the Standard of **Weights and Measures**;

To provide for the Punishment of counterfeiting the Securities and current Coin of the United States;

To establish **Post Offices** and post Roads;

To promote the Progress of **Science and useful Arts**, by securing for limited Times to Authors and Inventors the exclusive Right to their respective Writings and Discoveries; [patents and copyrights]

To **constitute Tribunals** inferior to the supreme Court;

To define and punish **Piracies and Felonies committed on the high Seas**, and Offences against the Law of Nations;

To **declare War**, grant Letters of Marque and Reprisal, and make Rules concerning Captures on Land and Water;

To **raise and support Armies**, but no Appropriation of Money to that Use shall be for a longer Term than two Years;

To provide and maintain a **Navy**;

To make Rules for the Government and Regulation of the **land and naval Forces**;

To provide for calling forth the Militia to execute the Laws of the Union, **suppress Insurrections and repel Invasions**;

To provide for **organizing, arming, and disciplining, the Militia**, and for governing such Part of them as may be employed in the Service of the United States, reserving to the States respectively, the Appointment of the Officers, and the Authority of training the Militia according to the discipline prescribed by Congress;

To exercise exclusive Legislation in all Cases whatsoever, over such District (not exceeding ten Miles square) as may, by Cession of particular States, and the Acceptance of Congress, become the **Seat of the Government of the United States**, and to exercise like Authority over all Places purchased by the Consent of the Legislature of the State in which the Same shall be, for the Erection of Forts, Magazines, Arsenals, dock-Yards, and other needful Buildings;—And

To make all **Laws which shall be necessary and proper** for carrying into Execution the foregoing Powers, and all other Powers vested by this Constitution in the Government of the United States, or in any Department or Officer thereof.

## Section 9.

The **Migration or Importation of such Persons** as any of the States now existing shall think proper to admit, shall not be prohibited by the Congress prior to the Year one thousand eight hundred and eight, but a Tax or duty may be imposed on such Importation, not exceeding ten dollars for each Person.

The Privilege of the **Writ of Habeas Corpus** shall not be suspended, unless when in Cases of Rebellion or Invasion the public Safety may require it.

No **Bill of Attainder** or **ex post facto Law** shall be passed.

No Capitation, or other direct, Tax shall be laid, <u>unless in Proportion to the Census or enumeration herein before directed to be taken</u>.

> [The underlined text in the preceding paragraph was replaced or affected by the 16th Amendment.]

No Tax or Duty shall be laid on Articles exported from any State.

No Preference shall be given by any **Regulation of Commerce or Revenue to the Ports** of one State over those of another: nor shall Vessels bound to, or from, one State, be obliged to enter, clear, or pay Duties in another.

No **Money shall be drawn from the Treasury**, but in Consequence of Appropriations made by Law; and a regular Statement and Account of the Receipts and Expenditures of all public Money shall be published from time to time.

**No Title of Nobility** shall be granted by the United States: And no Person holding any Office of Profit or Trust under them, shall, without the Consent of the Congress, accept of any present, **Emolument**, Office, or Title, of any kind whatever, from any King, Prince, or foreign State.

### Section 10.

**No State shall** enter into any **Treaty**, Alliance, or Confederation; grant Letters of Marque and Reprisal; **coin Money**; emit Bills of Credit; make any Thing but gold and silver Coin a Tender in Payment of Debts; pass any **Bill of Attainder**, **ex post facto Law**, or Law impairing the Obligation of Contracts, or grant any **Title of Nobility**.

**No State shall**, without the Consent of the Congress, lay any **Imposts or Duties** on Imports or Exports, except what may be absolutely necessary for executing it's inspection Laws: and the net Produce of all Duties and Imposts, laid by any State on Imports or Exports, shall be for the Use of the Treasury of the United States; and all such Laws shall be subject to the Revision and Controul of the Congress.

No State shall, without the Consent of Congress, lay any Duty of Tonnage, keep Troops, or Ships of War in time of Peace, enter into any Agreement or Compact with another State, or with a foreign Power, or engage in War, unless actually invaded, or in such imminent Danger as will not admit of delay.

### Article II

#### [Executive Branch: President, Vice President, etc.]

### Section 1.

The **executive Power shall be vested in a President** of the United States of America. He shall hold his Office during the

**Term of four Years**, and, together with the **Vice President**, chosen for the same Term, be elected, as follows

Each State shall appoint, in such Manner as the Legislature thereof may direct, a Number of Electors, equal to the whole Number of Senators and Representatives to which the State may be entitled in the Congress: but no Senator or Representative, or Person holding an Office of Trust or Profit under the United States, shall be appointed an Elector.

The Electors shall meet in their respective States, and vote by Ballot for two Persons, of whom one at least shall not be an Inhabitant of the same State with themselves. And they shall make a List of all the Persons voted for, and of the Number of Votes for each; which List they shall sign and certify, and transmit sealed to the Seat of the Government of the United States, directed to the President of the Senate. The President of the Senate shall, in the Presence of the Senate and House of Representatives, open all the Certificates, and the Votes shall then be counted. The Person having the greatest Number of Votes shall be the President, if such Number be a Majority of the whole Number of Electors appointed; and if there be more than one who have such Majority, and have an equal Number of Votes, then the House of Representatives shall immediately chuse by Ballot one of them for President; and if no Person have a Majority, then from the five highest on the List the said House shall in like Manner chuse the President. But in chusing the President, the Votes shall be taken by States, the Representation from each State having one Vote; A quorum for this Purpose shall consist of a Member or Members from two thirds of the States, and a Majority of all the States shall be necessary to a Choice. In every Case, after the Choice of the President, the Person having the greatest Number of Votes of the Electors shall be the Vice President. But if there should remain two or more who have equal Votes, the Senate shall chuse from them by Ballot the Vice President.

> [The underlined text in the preceding paragraph was replaced or affected by 12th Amendment.]

The Congress may determine the Time of chusing the Electors, and the **Day on which they shall give their Votes**; which Day shall be the same throughout the United States.

No Person except a **natural born Citizen**, or a Citizen of the United States, at the time of the Adoption of this Constitution, shall be eligible to the Office of President; neither shall any Person be eligible to that Office who shall not have attained to the **Age of thirty five Years**, and been **fourteen Years a Resident** within the United States.

In Case of the Removal of the President from Office, or of his Death, Resignation, or Inability to discharge the Powers and Duties of the said Office, the Same shall devolve on the Vice President, and the Congress may by Law provide for the Case of Removal, Death, Resignation or Inability, both of the President and Vice President, declaring what Officer shall then act as President, and such Officer shall act accordingly, until the Disability be removed, or a President shall be elected.

> [The underlined text in the preceding paragraph was replaced or affected by the 20th and 25th Amendments.]

The President shall, at stated Times, receive for his Services, a **Compensation**, which shall neither be encreased nor diminished during the Period for which he shall have been elected, and he shall not receive within that Period any other Emolument from the United States, or any of them.

Before he enter on the Execution of his Office, he shall take the following **Oath** or Affirmation:—"I do solemnly swear (or affirm) that I will faithfully execute the Office of President of the United States, and will to the best of my Ability, preserve, protect and defend the Constitution of the United States."

### Section 2.

The President shall be **Commander in Chief** of the Army and Navy of the United States, and of the Militia of the several States, when called into the actual Service of the United States; he may require the Opinion, in writing, of the principal Officer in each of the executive Departments, upon any Subject relating to the Duties of their respective Offices, and he shall have Power to grant Reprieves and **Pardons** for Offences against the United States, except in Cases of Impeachment.

He shall have Power, by and with the Advice and Consent of the Senate, to make **Treaties**, provided two thirds of the Senators present concur; and he shall nominate, and by and with the Advice and Consent of the Senate, shall appoint **Ambassadors**, other public Ministers and Consuls, **Judges** of the supreme Court, and all **other Officers** of the United States, whose Appointments are not herein otherwise provided for, and which shall be established by Law: but the Congress may by Law vest the Appointment of such inferior Officers, as they think proper, in the President alone, in the Courts of Law, or in the Heads of Departments.

The President shall have Power to **fill up all Vacancies** that may happen during the Recess of the Senate, by granting Commissions which shall expire at the End of their next Session.

### Section 3.

He shall from time to time give to the Congress Information of the **State of the Union**, and recommend to their Consideration such Measures as he shall judge necessary and expedient; he may, on extraordinary Occasions, **convene both Houses**, or either of them, and in Case of Disagreement between them, with Respect to the Time of Adjournment, he may adjourn them to such Time as he shall think proper; he shall receive Ambassadors and other public Ministers; he shall **take Care that the Laws be faithfully executed**, and shall Commission all the Officers of the United States.

### Section 4.

The President, Vice President and all civil Officers of the United States, shall be **removed from Office** on Impeachment for, and Conviction of, Treason, Bribery, or other high Crimes and Misdemeanors.

# Article III

## [Judicial Branch]

### Section 1.

The judicial Power of the United States, shall be vested in one **supreme Court**, and in such **inferior Courts** as the Congress may from time to time ordain and establish.

The **Judges**, both of the supreme and inferior Courts, shall hold their Offices **during good Behaviour**, and shall, at stated Times, receive for their Services, a **Compensation**, which shall not be diminished during their Continuance in Office.

### Section 2.

The **judicial Power shall extend to all Cases**, in Law and Equity, arising under this Constitution, the Laws of the United States, and Treaties made, or which shall be made, under their Authority;—to all Cases affecting Ambassadors, other public Ministers and Consuls;—to all Cases of admiralty and maritime Jurisdiction;—to Controversies to which the United States shall be a Party;—to Controversies between two or more States;— between a State and Citizens of another State,—between Citizens of different States,—between Citizens of the same State claiming Lands under Grants of different States, and between a State, or the Citizens thereof, and foreign States, Citizens or Subjects.

> [The underlined text in the preceding paragraph was replaced or affected by the 11th Amendment.]

In all Cases affecting Ambassadors, other public Ministers and Consuls, and those in which a State shall be Party, the supreme Court shall have **original Jurisdiction**. In all the other Cases before mentioned, the supreme Court shall have **appellate Jurisdiction**, both as to Law and Fact, with such Exceptions, and under such Regulations as the Congress shall make.

The Trial of all Crimes, except in Cases of Impeachment, shall be by **Jury**; and such Trial shall be held in the State where the said Crimes shall have been committed; but when not committed within any State, the Trial shall be at such Place or Places as the Congress may by Law have directed.

## Section 3.

**Treason** against the United States, shall consist only in levying War against them, or in adhering to their Enemies, giving them Aid and Comfort. No Person shall be convicted of Treason unless on the Testimony of two Witnesses to the same overt Act, or on Confession in open Court.

The Congress shall have Power to declare the **Punishment of Treason**, but no Attainder of Treason shall work Corruption of Blood, or Forfeiture except during the Life of the Person attainted.

## Article IV

### [Relations between states and their citizens]

## Section 1.

**Full Faith and Credit** shall be given in each State to the public Acts, Records, and judicial Proceedings of every other State. And the Congress may by general Laws prescribe the Manner in which such Acts, Records and Proceedings shall be proved, and the Effect thereof.

## Section 2.

The Citizens of each State shall be entitled to all **Privileges and Immunities** of Citizens in the several States.

A Person charged in any State with Treason, Felony, or other Crime, who shall flee from Justice, and be found in another State, shall on Demand of the executive Authority of the State from which he fled, be delivered up, to be removed to the State having Jurisdiction of the Crime.

No Person held to Service or Labour in one State, under the Laws thereof, escaping into another, shall, in Consequence of any Law or Regulation therein, be discharged from such Service or

<u>Labour, but shall be delivered up on Claim of the Party to whom such Service or Labour may be due.</u>

[The underlined text in the preceding paragraph was replaced or affected by the 13th Amendment.]

## Section 3.

**New States** may be admitted by the Congress into this Union; but no new State shall be formed or erected within the Jurisdiction of any other State; nor any State be formed by the Junction of two or more States, or Parts of States, without the Consent of the Legislatures of the States concerned as well as of the Congress.

The Congress shall have Power to dispose of and make all needful Rules and Regulations respecting the **Territory or other Property** belonging to the United States; and nothing in this Constitution shall be so construed as to Prejudice any Claims of the United States, or of any particular State.

## Section 4.

The United States shall guarantee to every State in this Union a **Republican Form of Government**, and shall **protect each of them against Invasion**; and on Application of the Legislature, or of the Executive (when the Legislature cannot be convened), against **domestic Violence**.

## Article V

### [How to amend the Constitution]

The Congress, whenever two thirds of both Houses shall deem it necessary, shall propose Amendments to this Constitution, or, on the Application of the Legislatures of two thirds of the several States, shall call a Convention for proposing Amendments, which, in either Case, shall be valid to all Intents and Purposes, as Part of this Constitution, when ratified by the Legislatures of three fourths of the several States, or by Conventions in three fourths thereof, as the one or the other Mode of Ratification may be proposed by the Congress; Provided that no Amendment which may be made prior to the Year One thousand eight hundred and eight shall in any Manner affect the first and fourth Clauses in the Ninth Section of the first Article; and that no State, without its Consent, shall be deprived of its equal Suffrage in the Senate.

## Article VI

### [Prior debts, supremacy of U.S. law, oaths of office, no religious tests]

All **Debts** contracted and Engagements entered into, before the Adoption of this Constitution, shall be as valid against the United States under this Constitution, as under the Confederation.

This Constitution, and the Laws of the United States which shall be made in Pursuance thereof; and all Treaties made, or which shall be made, under the Authority of the United States, shall be the **supreme Law of the Land**; and the Judges in every State shall be bound thereby, any Thing in the Constitution or Laws of any State to the Contrary notwithstanding.

The Senators and Representatives before mentioned, and the Members of the several State Legislatures, and all executive and judicial Officers, both of the United States and of the several States, shall be bound by **Oath** or Affirmation, to support this Constitution; but no religious Test shall ever be required as a Qualification to any Office or public Trust under the United States.

## Article VII

### [Ratification of the Constitution]

The Ratification of the Conventions of nine States, shall be sufficient for the Establishment of this Constitution between the States so ratifying the Same.

The Word, "the," being interlined between the seventh and eighth Lines of the first Page, The Word "Thirty" being partly written on an Erazure in the fifteenth Line of the first Page, The Words "is tried" being interlined between the thirty second and thirty third

Lines of the first Page and the Word "the" being interlined between the forty third and forty fourth Lines of the second Page.

Attest William Jackson Secretary

done in Convention by the Unanimous Consent of the States present **the Seventeenth Day of September in the Year of our Lord one thousand seven hundred and Eighty seven** and of the Independance of the United States of America the Twelfth In witness whereof We have hereunto subscribed our Names,

**[Signers' names omitted: check online]**

## AMENDMENTS TO THE CONSTITUTION

### [Preamble omitted]

[**Bill of Rights** is first 10 Amendments, ratified in 1791]

### Amendment I [1st]

Congress shall make no law respecting an establishment of **religion**, or prohibiting the free exercise thereof; or abridging the **freedom of speech**, or of **the press**; or the right of the people **peaceably to assemble**, and to **petition the Government** for a redress of grievances.

### Amendment II [2nd]

A well regulated Militia, being necessary to the security of a free State, the right of the people to **keep and bear Arms**, shall not be infringed.

### Amendment III [3rd]

**No Soldier** shall, in time of peace **be quartered** in any house, without the consent of the Owner, nor in time of war, but in a manner to be prescribed by law.

### Amendment IV [4th]

The right of the people to be secure in their persons, houses, papers, and effects, against **unreasonable searches and**

**seizures**, shall not be violated, and no **Warrants** shall issue, but upon probable cause, supported by Oath or affirmation, and particularly describing the place to be searched, and the persons or things to be seized.

## Amendment V [5th]

No person shall be held to answer for a capital, or otherwise infamous **crime**, unless on a presentment or indictment of a **Grand Jury**, except in cases arising in the land or naval forces, or in the Militia, when in actual service in time of War or public danger; nor shall any person be subject for the same offence to be **twice put in jeopardy** of life or limb; nor shall be compelled in any criminal case to be a **witness against himself**, nor be deprived of life, liberty, or property, without **due process of law**; nor shall **private property** be taken for public use, without just compensation.

## Amendment VI [6th]

In all **criminal prosecutions**, the accused shall enjoy the right to a **speedy and public trial**, by an **impartial jury** of the State and district wherein the crime shall have been committed, which district shall have been previously ascertained by law, and to be informed of the nature and cause of the accusation; to be **confronted with the witnesses** against him; to have **compulsory process for obtaining witnesses** in his favor, and to have the **Assistance of Counsel** for his defence.

## Amendment VII [7th]

In **Suits at common law**, where the value in controversy shall exceed twenty dollars, the right of **trial by jury** shall be preserved, and no fact tried by a jury, shall be otherwise re-examined in any Court of the United States, than according to the rules of the common law.

## Amendment VIII [8th]

Excessive **bail** shall not be required, nor excessive **fines** imposed, nor **cruel and unusual punishments** inflicted.

## Amendment IX [9th]

The enumeration in the Constitution, of certain rights, shall not be construed to deny or disparage others retained by the people.

## Amendment X [10th]

The **powers** not delegated to the United States by the Constitution, nor prohibited by it to the States, are **reserved to the States** respectively, or to the people.

# OTHER AMENDMENTS

## Amendment XI [11th, ratified 1795]

The Judicial power of the United States shall not be construed to extend to any suit in law or equity, commenced or prosecuted against one of the United States by Citizens of another State, or by Citizens or Subjects of any Foreign State.

## Amendment XII [12th, ratified 1804]

The Electors shall meet in their respective states and vote by **ballot for President and Vice-President**, one of whom, at least, shall not be an inhabitant of the same state with themselves; they shall name in their ballots the person voted for as President, and in distinct ballots the person voted for as Vice-President, and they shall make distinct lists of all persons voted for as President, and of all persons voted for as Vice-President, and of the number of votes for each, which lists they shall sign and certify, and transmit sealed to the seat of the government of the United States, directed to the President of the Senate; -- the President of the Senate shall, in the presence of the Senate and House of Representatives, open all the certificates and the votes shall then be counted; -- The person having the greatest number of votes for President, shall be the President, if such number be a majority of the whole number of Electors appointed; and if no person have such majority, then from the persons having the highest numbers not exceeding three on the list of those voted for as President, the House of Representatives shall choose immediately, by ballot, the President.

But in choosing the President, the votes shall be taken by states, the representation from each state having one vote; a quorum for this purpose shall consist of a member or members from two-thirds of the states, and a majority of all the states shall be necessary to a choice. And if the House of Representatives shall not choose a President whenever the right of choice shall devolve upon them, before the fourth day of March next following, then the Vice-President shall act as President, as in case of the death or other constitutional disability of the President. -- The person having the greatest number of votes as Vice-President, shall be the Vice-President, if such number be a majority of the whole number of Electors appointed, and if no person have a majority, then from the two highest numbers on the list, the Senate shall choose the Vice-President; a quorum for the purpose shall consist of two-thirds of the whole number of Senators, and a majority of the whole number shall be necessary to a choice. But no person constitutionally ineligible to the office of President shall be eligible to that of Vice-President of the United States.

[The underlined text in the preceding paragraph was replaced or affected by 20th Amendment.]

## Amendment XIII [13th, ratified 1865]

**Section 1**. Neither **slavery** nor involuntary servitude, except as a punishment for crime whereof the party shall have been duly convicted, shall exist within the United States, or any place subject to their jurisdiction.

**Section 2**. Congress shall have power to enforce this article by appropriate legislation.

## Amendment XIV [14th, ratified in 1868]

**Section 1**. All persons born or naturalized in the United States, and subject to the jurisdiction thereof, are citizens of the United States and of the State wherein they reside. No State shall make or enforce any law which shall abridge the **privileges or immunities of citizens** of the United States; nor shall any State deprive any person of life, liberty, or property, without **due**

**process of law**; nor deny to any person within its jurisdiction the **equal protection** of the laws.

**Section 2**. Representatives shall be apportioned among the several States according to their respective numbers, counting the whole number of persons in each State, excluding Indians not taxed. But when the **right to vote** at any election for the choice of electors for President and Vice-President of the United States, Representatives in Congress, the Executive and Judicial officers of a State, or the members of the Legislature thereof, is denied to any of the **male** inhabitants of such State, being twenty-one years of age, and citizens of the United States, or in any way abridged, except for participation in rebellion, or other crime, the basis of representation therein shall be reduced in the proportion which the number of such male citizens shall bear to the whole number of male citizens twenty-one years of age in such State.

[The underlined text in the preceding paragraph was replaced or affected by 26th Amendment.]

**Section 3**. No person shall be a Senator or Representative in Congress, or elector of President and Vice-President, or hold any office, civil or military, under the United States, or under any State, who, having previously taken an oath, as a member of Congress, or as an officer of the United States, or as a member of any State legislature, or as an executive or judicial officer of any State, to support the Constitution of the United States, shall have engaged in insurrection or rebellion against the same, or given aid or comfort to the enemies thereof. But Congress may by a vote of two-thirds of each House, remove such disability.

**Section 4**. The validity of the **public debt** of the United States, authorized by law, including debts incurred for payment of pensions and bounties for services in suppressing insurrection or rebellion, shall not be questioned. But neither the United States nor any State shall assume or pay any debt or obligation incurred in aid of insurrection or rebellion against the United States, or any claim for the loss or emancipation of any slave; but all such debts, obligations and claims shall be held illegal and void.

**Section 5**. The Congress shall have the **power to enforce**, by appropriate legislation, the provisions of this article.

### Amendment XV [15th, ratified 1870]

**Section 1**. The right of citizens of the United States to **vote** shall not be denied or abridged by the United States or by any State on account of **race, color,** or previous condition of servitude—

**Section 2**. The Congress shall have the **power to enforce** this article by appropriate legislation.

### Amendment XVI [16th, ratified 1913]

The Congress shall have power to lay and collect **taxes on incomes**, from whatever source derived, without apportionment among the several States, and without regard to any census or enumeration.

### Amendment XVII [17th, ratified 1913]

The Senate of the United States shall be composed of two **Senators** from each State, **elected by the people** thereof, for six years; and each Senator shall have one vote. The electors in each State shall have the qualifications requisite for electors of the most numerous branch of the State legislatures.

When **vacancies** happen in the representation of any State **in the Senate**, the executive authority of such State shall issue writs of election to fill such vacancies: Provided, That the legislature of any State may empower the executive thereof to make temporary appointments until the people fill the vacancies by election as the legislature may direct.

This amendment shall not be so construed as to affect the election or term of any Senator chosen before it becomes valid as part of the Constitution

### Amendment XVIII [18th, ratified 1919]

**Section 1**. After one year from the ratification of this article the manufacture, sale, or transportation of **intoxicating liquors** within, the importation thereof into, or the exportation thereof from the United States and all territory subject to the jurisdiction thereof for beverage purposes is hereby prohibited.

**Section 2**. The Congress and the several States shall have concurrent power to enforce this article by appropriate legislation.

**Section 3**. This article shall be inoperative unless it shall have been ratified as an amendment to the Constitution by the legislatures of the several States, as provided in the Constitution, within seven years from the date of the submission hereof to the States by the Congress.

[The 18th Amendment was repealed by the 21st Amendment]

## Amendment XIX [19th, ratified 1920]

The right of citizens of the United States to **vote** shall not be denied or abridged by the United States or by any State on account of **sex**.

Congress shall have **power to enforce** this article by appropriate legislation.

## Amendment XX [20th, ratified 1933]

**Section 1**. The **terms** of the President and the Vice President shall end at noon on the 20th day of January, and the terms of Senators and Representatives at noon on the 3d day of January, of the years in which such terms would have ended if this article had not been ratified; and the terms of their successors shall then begin.

**Section 2**. The **Congress shall assemble** at least once in every year, and such meeting shall begin at noon on the 3d day of January, unless they shall by law appoint a different day.

**Section 3**. **If**, at the time fixed for the beginning of the term of the President, **the President elect shall have died**, the Vice President elect shall become President. If a President shall not have been chosen before the time fixed for the beginning of his term, or if the President elect shall have failed to qualify, then the

Vice President elect shall act as President until a President shall
have qualified; and the Congress may by law provide for the case
wherein neither a President elect nor a Vice President elect shall
have qualified, declaring who shall then act as President, or the
manner in which one who is to act shall be selected, and such
person shall act accordingly until a President or Vice President
shall have qualified.

**Section 4.** The Congress may by law provide for the case
of the death of any of the persons from whom the House of
Representatives may choose a President whenever the right of
choice shall have devolved upon them, and for the case of the
death of any of the persons from whom the Senate may choose a
Vice President whenever the right of choice shall have devolved
upon them.

**Section 5.** Sections 1 and 2 shall take effect on the 15th day of
October following the ratification of this article.

**Section 6.** This article shall be inoperative unless it shall have
been ratified as an amendment to the Constitution by the
legislatures of three-fourths of the several States within seven
years from the date of its submission.

### Amendment XXI [21st, ratified 1933]

**Section 1.** The **eighteenth** article of **amendment** to the
Constitution of the United States is hereby **repealed**.

**Section 2.** The transportation or importation into any State,
Territory, or possession of the United States for delivery or use
therein of **intoxicating liquors**, in violation of the laws thereof, is
hereby prohibited.

**Section 3.** This article shall be inoperative unless it shall
have been ratified as an amendment to the Constitution by
conventions in the several States, as provided in the Constitution,
within seven years from the date of the submission hereof to the
States by the Congress.

## Amendment XXII [22nd, ratified 1951]

**Section 1**. No person shall be **elected to the office of the President more than twice**, and no person who has held the office of President, or acted as President, for more than two years of a term to which some other person was elected President shall be elected to the office of the President more than once. But this Article shall not apply to any person holding the office of President when this Article was proposed by the Congress, and shall not prevent any person who may be holding the office of President, or acting as President, during the term within which this Article becomes operative from holding the office of President or acting as President during the remainder of such term.

**Section 2**. This article shall be inoperative unless it shall have been ratified as an amendment to the Constitution by the legislatures of three-fourths of the several States within seven years from the date of its submission to the States by the Congress.

## Amendment XXIII [23rd, ratified 1961]

**Section 1**. The **District** [Washington D.C.] constituting the seat of Government of the United States shall appoint in such manner as the Congress may direct: A number of **electors of President and Vice President** equal to the whole number of Senators and Representatives in Congress to which the District would be entitled if it were a State, but in no event more than the least populous State; they shall be in addition to those appointed by the States, but they shall be considered, for the purposes of the election of President and Vice President, to be electors appointed by a State; and they shall meet in the District and perform such duties as provided by the twelfth article of amendment.

**Section 2**. The Congress shall have **power to enforce** this article by appropriate legislation.

## Amendment XXIV [24th, ratified 1964]

**Section 1**. The **right** of citizens of the United States **to vote** in any primary or other election for President or Vice President, for electors for President or Vice President, or for Senator or Representative in Congress, shall not be denied or abridged by the United States or any State by reason of failure to pay any **poll tax** or other tax.

**Section 2**. The Congress shall have **power to enforce** this article by appropriate legislation.

## Amendment XXV [25th, ratified 1967]

**Section 1**. In case of the **removal of the President** from office or of his death or resignation, the Vice President shall become President.

**Section 2**. Whenever there is a **vacancy in the office of the Vice President**, the President shall nominate a Vice President who shall take office upon confirmation by a majority vote of both Houses of Congress.

**Section 3**. Whenever the **President** transmits to the President pro tempore of the Senate and the Speaker of the House of Representatives his written declaration that he is **unable to discharge the powers and duties** of his office, and until he transmits to them a written declaration to the contrary, such powers and duties shall be discharged by the Vice President as Acting President.

**Section 4**. Whenever the **Vice President and a majority of either the principal officers** of the executive departments or of such other body as Congress may by law provide, transmit to the President pro tempore of the Senate and the Speaker of the House of Representatives their written declaration that the **President is unable** to discharge the powers and duties of his office, the Vice President shall immediately assume the powers and duties of the office as Acting President.

Thereafter, when the **President** transmits to the President pro tempore of the Senate and the Speaker of the House of Representatives his written declaration that no inability exists, he shall **resume the powers and duties** of his office unless the Vice President and a majority of either the principal officers of the executive department or of such other body as Congress may by law provide, transmit within four days to the President pro tempore of the Senate and the Speaker of the House of Representatives their written declaration that the President is unable to discharge the powers and duties of his office. Thereupon Congress shall decide the issue, assembling within forty-eight hours for that purpose if not in session. If the Congress, within twenty-one days after receipt of the latter written declaration, or, if Congress is not in session, within twenty-one days after Congress is required to assemble, determines by two-thirds vote of both Houses that the President is unable to discharge the powers and duties of his office, the Vice President shall continue to discharge the same as Acting President; otherwise, the President shall resume the powers and duties of his office.

## Amendment XXVI [26th, ratified 1971]

**Section 1**. The right of citizens of the United States, who are **eighteen years of age** or older, to **vote** shall not be denied or abridged by the United States or by any State on account of age.

**Section 2**. The Congress shall have **power to enforce** this article by appropriate legislation.

## Amendment XXVII [27th, ratified 1992]

No law, varying the **compensation** for the services of the **Senators** and **Representatives**, shall take effect, until an election of Representatives shall have intervened.

# Index

CPSIA information can be obtained
at www.ICGtesting.com
Printed in the USA
LVHW03s0209150618
580751LV00003B/558/P